# SELF-FULFILLING PROPHECY

# SELF-FULFILLING PROPHECY

## A Practical Guide
## to Its Use in Education

ROBERT T. TAUBER

PRAEGER

Westport, Connecticut
London

**Library of Congress Cataloging-in-Publication Data**

Tauber, Robert T.
   Self-fulfilling prophecy : a practical guide to its use in
education / Robert T. Tauber.
     p.    cm.
   Includes bibliographical references and index.
   ISBN 0–275–95502–8 (alk. paper).—ISBN 0–275–95503–6 (pbk. :
alk. paper)
    1. Teacher-student relationships—United States.  2. Self-
fulfilling prophecy.  3. Teachers—Psychology.  4. Multicultural
education—United States.  I. Title.
LB1033.T19   1997
371.1′023—dc20       96–33192

British Library Cataloguing in Publication Data is available

Library of Congress Catalog Card Number: 96–33192
ISBN: 0–275–95502–8
     0–275–95503–6 (pbk.)

First published in 1997

Praeger Publishers, 88 Post Road West, Westport, CT 06881
An imprint of Greenwood Publishing Group, Inc.

Printed in the United States of America

The paper used in this book complies with the
Permanent Paper Standard issued by the National
Information Standards Organization (Z39.48–1984).

10 9 8 7 6 5 4 3 2 1

# CONTENTS

# ILLUSTRATIONS

# PREFACE

Too often what we expect is exactly what we get. Nowhere is this more true than in education, where teachers' expectations of students are crucial. The self-fulfilling prophecy (SFP), therefore, should be of great interest to teachers, both those in training and those in service.

Whether or not a teacher is aware of it, the SFP is at work, impacting students either to their benefit or their detriment. It follows, then, that teachers should be made aware of the SFP and how it can be used effectively in education. This is the goal of this book.

For teachers in training, the SFP should be addressed in a variety of required teacher education courses including, but not limited to, Educational Psychology, Developmental Psychology, Secondary Teaching Methods, and Elementary Teaching Methods. For student teachers, the SFP should be addressed in seminars that accompany their semester-long practicum. For in-service teachers, the SFP should be dealt with via a variety of ongoing professional development endeavors—induction year programs, inservice offerings, graduate study, professional conferences, and so forth.

This study of the SFP also is appropriate for undergraduate special education, diversity, and multicultural courses (a current emphasis in most colleges and universities), as well as for graduate-level administrative, special education, supervisory, and counseling and guidance courses.

Today, perhaps more than ever before, educators are finding themselves teaching students who are very different from themselves. Those most likely to pursue a teaching career—white, Anglo-Saxon, average or above in intelligence, middle-class, females—are entering very diverse classrooms. For instance, urban schools are likely to have a high concentration of minorities—as defined by race and ethnicity. Special children, once segregated to physically handicapped and/or emotionally disturbed classes, now are mainstreamed into "regular" classrooms.

More and more students are enrolled in votech-type programs where their time and interests are shared between their trade and their academics. Many schools regularly find themselves filled with students, from inner-city residents to recent immigrants, who have English as a second language. Nontraditional adult students also are appearing in classrooms in increasing numbers. All of these various and sundry student bodies can present a special challenge.

Teachers must cope. In order to cope effectively with a growing student body that differs from themselves, teachers must recognize, understand, and then control the expectations they bring to the classroom.

One way to gauge the timeliness of the contents of this book is to examine how often the subject of the self-fulfilling prophecy appears in the title of education-oriented publications. A CD-ROM search of ERIC (Educational Resources Information Center) from 1983 to 1995 reveals 798 article titles containing the term "expectations"—the basis of the SFP. The same search reveals over 100 citations with the words "expectations" and "teacher" in the articles' titles.

A CD-ROM search of ERIC's Word/Phrase Index using the key words "expectation," "expectation effects," "expectation (psychology)," or "expectations" reveals over 7,900 *CIJE* (*Current Index to Journals in Education*) and *RIE* (*Resources in Education*) citations. The majority of these deal with school-related expectations by teachers, peers, and parents. Note that ERIC is described in detail in chapter 16.

Clearly, the self-fulfilling prophecy, as evidenced by the large number of articles, documents, and dissertations written on the topic of "expectations," is of great and continuing interest to educators at all levels.

If educators themselves were to obtain and read the many journal articles and doctoral dissertations dealing with the subject of the self-fulfilling prophecy, there would be no need for this book. But the fact is that most busy educators, whether preservice or in-service, either may not possess the skill and/or means to secure these resources or, if obtained, may lack the time and energy to wade through them all. Hence, the need for this book.

Although the official title of this book is *Self-Fulfilling Prophecy: A Practical Guide to Its Use in Education*, its use is not limited to just education (i.e., kindergarten through 12th grade). Anywhere and anytime two or more people get together, expectations are formed and hence the self-fulfilling prophecy is activated. The contents of this book, therefore, apply to the armed services, homes, businesses, industry, marriages, and so forth.

# ACKNOWLEDGMENTS

To Cecelia Anne, my wife and very best friend, who has exceeded even my wildest expectations, to David Madison and Rebecca Anne, our children, who we predict will continue to exceed our expectations, and to all those Pygmalions in my life, especially my mother and father, without whom I never would have succeeded, thank you.

To Wendy Eidenmuller, a special friend and division secretary, who without her untiring services little or none of my work would ever make it to press, thank you.

\*\*\*\*\*

To Sheila Feathers, a special friend (in memory), we expected a lot from you, and you gave us so much more. We miss you.

# SELF-FULFILLING PROPHECY

# PART I

# SFP MECHANISMS

Following an introduction to the self-fulfilling prophecy (SFP) in chapter 1, the step-by-step mechanics of the SFP process are presented in chapter 2. Chapter 3 ends this portion of the book by noting that the SFP is a worldwide phenomenon.

# CHAPTER 1

# INTRODUCTION

*The ultimate function of a prophecy is not to tell the future, but to make it.*
—Wagar (1963, p. 66)

## INTRODUCTION

How many of you think that you are a reasonably good judge of character? With years of experience under your belt, are you more often than not able to size up people correctly? Sure, occasionally you are wrong, but most often you are correct. Right? Most people believe that they can tell—sometimes at just a glance—just how certain kinds of people they come in contact with are likely to act.

Do you ever catch yourself, or do you overhear others, saying such things as, "Look, here comes so and so, just look at how he is dressed! He's just a big show-off, don't you think?" or "Look who just pulled up in her new flashy car. She's really stuck on herself, isn't she?" In both of these scenarios, each person in question has had his or her basic personality sized up according to the clothes he wears or the car she drives. Once he has been pegged as a show-off or she has been labeled as "stuck up," then "evidence" to support these assertions will be sought. Without even realizing it, the self-fulfilling prophecy is off and running.

## OPENING EXERCISE

We all know what certain people are like, don't we? Granted, all of "them" (i.e., flashy dressers) are not like that, but, generally, most of "them" are. Everyone knows basically that this is a fact! It's just how "they" are." Sounds like a "Seinfeld" show dialogue between Jerry Seinfeld and his friend George Kostanza, doesn't it?

Even though there may be some of "these" people who are exceptions to the rule, you probably know what the prevailing view is about "these" kinds of people. Once in a while one or two of "them" will prove you to be wrong, but most of the time you can just about tell ahead of time how "they" are going to act—can't you? With this view in mind, complete the following exercise. This exercise follows a "free-response approach" rather than an "adjective checklist approach." The difference between these two data collection methods is that in the former, subjects are asked to describe various groups' stereotypical behavior without putting words into their mouths or at the tips of their pencils as is the case with adjective checklists.

### Directions

Here are some labels that categorize different kinds of *those* people. Take out a sheet of paper and jot down the first descriptive thoughts that come to your mind when you think about *these* kinds of people. Be honest, now; no one but you will see what you write.

Generally, what descriptors would most people offer when asked to characterize:

A "jock" taking an introductory history course

A significantly overweight (fat) girl

A cheerleader

An engineering student

A minority woman with four kids at the market using food stamps

A Hispanic

An A.M. (versus P.M.) kindergarten child

A person standing outside smoking on a cold February day

Even though your written responses may not represent your personal views about these kinds of people, the majority of the time, stereotypical descriptions emerge from this exercise. This tells us, generally, that there is a prevailing view commonly held by respondents. Does this prevailing view, then, influence how these kinds of people are treated? By and large, the self-fulfilling prophecy (SFP) would say yes!

How are these kinds of people viewed? An informal anonymous survey of primarily middle-class, white undergraduate students taking a Management of Interpersonal Relationships course, most of whom were Education, Psychology, or Management majors from a small college within a larger university system, generated the following responses to these kinds of people. Compare their comments to the ones that you wrote.

A "jock" taking an introductory history class
  1. Someone else doing his homework, lazy
  2. A big guy who isn't very intelligent
  3. Aspiring for something more than sports
  4. Taking it for the credits—not really interested in class
  5. Underachiever, loves to party
  6. Stupid
  7. Disinterested, if he understands it at all
  8. Not interested
  9. Struggling to understand the syllabus
 10. Athlete, dedicated, interested in learning
 11. The jock is dumb
 12. Probably not going to do well
 13. Kiss-up for a grade
 14. Slow person sleeping through class
 15. Passing—barely getting by
 16. A student filling a general education requirement
 17. Slackers, not too bright, care more about sports
 18. Has test file from fraternity, just getting a passing grade
 19. Think about their sport during class
 20. Needs it just to be able to keep up his GPA to play sport

A significantly overweight (fat) girl
  1. Sad, unhappy with herself, no friends
  2. A person who is sloppy and eats a lot
  3. Low self-esteem
  4. Lacking something in her life, missing something
  5. Lonely, depressed
  6. Quiet
  7. Lazy, sloppy, depressed, doesn't care about herself
  8. Unhappy
  9. Low self-esteem, quiet, eats a lot
 10. Nothing specific comes to mind
 11. Nice personality
 12. Lazy
 13. Eats a lot, dirty, gross
 14. Has a hormone problem, just doesn't take care of herself
 15. Low self-esteem
 16. Someone with "eating disorder" thyroid problem

17. Nice person
18. Unliked, close to her mother
19. Doesn't take care of her body or has a medical problem
20. Someone who might have low self-esteem and eats a great deal

A cheerleader
   1. Brain-dead Barbie doll
   2. Someone who is stupid, dumb sport
   3. Peppy and cheerful
   4. Has a lot of spirit, usually kind of peppy
   5. Flighty, dumb blond, laughs a lot
   6. Popular, bouncy
   7. Brainless; social butterfly
   8. Think they're better than anyone else
   9. Air heads, study with the jocks for history
10. Social, spirited, definitely not an Einstein
11. Attractive, but unintelligent
12. Stupid
13. Snob
14. Ditz, blonde, bubbly, loud
15. Dumb
16. Someone filled to the brim with pep
17. Ditzy, pretty, thin, stuck-up
18. Blonde, ditzy, naive
19. Jumpy, hyper, talks a lot
20. Someone who is very personable

An engineering student
   1. Book smart no common sense
   2. Someone who is very intelligent
   3. Extremely devoted and intelligent
   4. Smart, good with numbers
   5. Very smart
   6. Studious
   7. Serious-minded students, logical
   8. Motivated to finish course and do well
   9. Very logical, don't laugh too often
10. Smart, scientific, not social, analytical, boring
11. Intelligent, pays attention to detail
12. Bright, goal oriented

13. Hard worker, sometimes a little nerdy
14. Skinny little, nerdy math whiz
15. Very intelligent
16. Wears a plastic pocket protector filled with pens
17. Intelligent, math students
18. Drives a truck, owns a gun rack, chews tobacco
19. Thinks logically
20. Someone who is intelligent and likes to think in math terms

A minority woman with four kids at the market using food stamps
 1. Welfare leach, lazy, not married
 2. Someone who doesn't want to work so she depends on welfare
 3. Disadvantaged, possibly lazy
 4. Doesn't have a lot of money—on government assistance
 5. Inner city, bad environment
 6. Low-life
 7. Single, on welfare, all the kids have different fathers
 8. Poverty
 9. Had the kids to get more welfare
10. Low income, single parent, welfare
11. Loser on welfare without husband
12. Lazy, no pride
13. Welfare, single mom, lives in ghetto
14. Lazy, abuses the welfare system
15. Welfare, low intelligence
16. Someone who is unable to support herself and her children
17. Lazy, no job, but yet cares about her children
18. Welfare mother, unmarried, undisciplined, irresponsible
19. She may be having kids to continue receiving welfare
20. Someone who was left by a man and can't get a job

A Hispanic
 1. Foreigner, can't speak English
 2. Slow moving
 3. Festive
 4. A lot of lower jobs—More and more immigrating into U.S.
 5. Gang member, drug dealer
 6. Chatty
 7. Stereotyped as stupid; poor; short-tempered
 8. Laborers—population increasing

9. Troublemakers, stick to their own
10. Spanish—that's all I think of
11. No opinion
12. Won't learn the language
13. Dirty
14. Bad taste in clothes, jewelry, and cars
15. Lazy
16. Someone of Latino heritage
17. Temperamental
18. Flamboyant, loud, violent
19. Fast talking
20. Someone who works in our country and tends to be lazy

An A.M. (versus P.M.) kindergarten child
 1. Very early riser, eager to learn and alert
 2. That they are morning kids
 3. A morning person, hard worker
 4. May be motivated to work more in morning later in life
 5. Rowdy
 6. Tired
 7. Smarter, better attention spans because they are more alert
 8. Both parents probably work
 9. Have to get moving early
10. Efficient parents, prompt, task oriented, motivated
11. Parents work first shift
12. Single parent
13. Wants to get a jump on life
14. Their parents have higher expectations for them
15. Very productive
16. A child whose parents are both employed
17. Like to be at school early
18. Smarter, brighter, more creative
19. Their parents want them to get in the habit of waking up
20. A kid who can get up in the morning and is anxious to learn

A person standing outside smoking on a cold February day
 1. Hooked, having a nicotine fit
 2. Someone who needs a smoke
 3. Addicted wanna-be's
 4. Idiots, need help but are unwilling to get it

5. Chain smokers, stressed out

6. Die-hards—literally

7. Too psychologically & physically addicted to have any sense

8. Crazy

9. Nicotine is more important than their health

10. Addicts

11. They are addicted to nicotine

12. Weak, lets dirty habit control them

13. Stressed, stupid

14. They're absolutely pathetic

15. Idiots

16. People addicted to nicotine and maybe stressed out

17. Chain smokers, show-offs

18. Helplessly needy and dependent

19. They are so desperate they go out in the cold just to smoke

20. Someone who has a nasty unbreakable habit

Just a thought. Pity someone who is an overweight, Hispanic, female cheerleader who uses food stamps, and who is standing outside on a cold February morning smoking! I am not sure that we could print how the world might view this kind of person! Like it or not, there are people out there forming just these kinds of judgments about others. Often, these "others" are children who are in a poor position to resist these damning expectations.

Like beauty, expectations are in the eye of the beholder. Therefore, try out this list on several other people and see what their "eyes" behold. What do they expect from these kinds of people? Do their expectations reflect yours? Do they reflect those shown above? Once the expectations have been formed, can differential behaviors be far away? The self-fulfilling prophecy answer is no! Teachers expect students identified as being part of a "fast group" or a "slow group" to perform consistently with that characteristic (Saracho, 1991).

## HISTORY OF THE SELF-FULFILLING PROPHECY

The term "self-fulfilling prophecy" was first coined by sociologist Robert K. Merton in a 1948 *Antioch Review* article titled "The Self-Fulfilling Prophecy." As part of his explanation of the self-fulfilling prophecy, Merton drew upon a fellow sociologist's theorem: "If men define situations as real, they are real in their consequences" (Thomas, 1928, p. 527). According to Merton (1948), "The self-fulfilling prophecy is, in the beginning, a *false* definition of the situation evoking a new behavior which makes the originally false conception come *true*. The specious validity of the self-fulfilling prophecy perpetuates a reign of error. For the prophet will cite the actual course of events as proof that he was right from the very beginning" (p. 195).

Although Merton did not apply the concept and mechanics of the self-fulfilling prophecy to classrooms specifically, the potential for use (and abuse) of the self-fulfilling prophecy in schools can be generalized easily. In discussing real-world examples of the self-fulfilling prophecy (e.g., world of banking, race relations), Merton offered the surprising caution not to rely upon the education community to cure social problems—including the tragic, often vicious, circle of the self-fulfilling prophecy. He argued that, like other Americans, teachers share the very prejudices (expectations) they would be asked to combat (Merton, 1948).

In an often-cited study, Rosenthal and Fode (1963), and later Rosenthal and Lawson (1964), set out to test the hypothesis that experimenters are able to obtain from their animal subjects the results they expect to obtain. Although the term "self-fulfilling prophecy" was not used in the study, all of the ingredients of the SFP were present—manipulated expectations of student experimenters, differential treatment of the subject rats by the experimenters, and realized or fulfilled expectations of experimenters.

In this study, experimental psychology students were given one of two types of rats, designated "maze-dull" or "maze-bright," to run through a series of T-maze experiments. Students with the maze-bright rats were told that the rats would perform normally at first, but thereafter, their performance would increase markedly. The students with the maze-dull rats were told that their rats were not expected to show much evidence of learning. In reality, the rats had been assigned to student experimenters on a random basis—any differences among the rats existed only in the student experimenters' expectations.

By the end of the five-day study, the maze-bright rats had, in fact, performed significantly better. Perhaps more important than how well the rats actually performed was how the student handlers rated (described) the rats and their own behavior. Maze-bright handlers rated their rats more favorably (e.g., brighter, tamer, and more pleasant) and themselves more favorably (e.g., more relaxed) than did the maze-dull rat handlers.

The attention of educators to the self-fulfilling prophecy and to its possible negative impact upon schoolchildren, as opposed to just laboratory mice, occurred when Rosenthal and Jacobson published their eye-opening article in *Scientific American* titled "Teacher Expectations for the Disadvantaged" (1968b). The alarming message of this scholarly publication was made more widely available to education practitioners via Rosenthal and Jacobson's book, *Pygmalion in the Classroom* (1968a).

The word "Pygmalion" comes from mythology; Pygmalion was a sculptor who set about sculpting an ivory statue of the perfect woman. While doing so, he fell in love with his creation and longed for it to become real. Aphrodite, the goddess of love, feeling sorry for Pygmalion, allowed the statue to come to life. The sculpture's wish was fulfilled.

In George Bernard Shaw's play *Pygmalion* and in *My Fair Lady*, as well as the Broadway musical that became a movie, Professor Higgins (played by Rex Harrison), a modern-day Pygmalion, transforms a Covenant Gardens (London) screeching, crude, and boisterous flower girl (played by Julie Andrews in the play) into a confident, refined, and charming lady—in fact, a princess. "Important to the concept of the self-fulfilling prophecy is that the flower girl became what the professor expected her to become" (Roach & Arnold, 1991, p. 40). In the end, Eliza Doolittle proclaims, "The difference between a flower lady and a princess is not how she acts, but how she is treated"—the essence of the self-fulfilling prophecy.

In their now classic mid-1960s study, Robert Rosenthal, a Harvard University researcher, and Lenore Jacobson, the principal of the elementary school where the research was conducted, manipulated the expectations of the school's teachers (Rosenthal & Jacobson, 1966). The two researchers, presumably using the results from a test with the impressive title Harvard Test of Inflected Acquisition, which had been administered schoolwide, led the teachers in eighteen classrooms to believe that approximately 20% of their students were expected to "bloom" academically and intellectually during the school year. The test that was administered was, in reality, a relatively new intelligence test titled the Flanagan Test of General Ability.

The test results, of course, were never actually the basis for identifying which students were designated to bloom. Instead, the designated student "bloomers" were randomly assigned so that the only differences between the bloomers (the equivalent of the experimental group) and the rest of the student body (the equivalent of the experimental control) were in the minds of the teachers. When retested later using the same intelligence test, the designated bloomers or spurters did, in fact, show intellectual gains!

At the end of the academic school year, when asked to describe the classroom behavior of their students, the children from whom intellectual growth was expected (i.e., designated "bloomers") were described by their teachers as having a greater chance of being more successful in later life, as being happier, more curious, more interesting, more appealing, better adjusted, and more affectionate than the other students (Rosenthal & Jacobson, 1968b). Although for ethical reasons Rosenthal and Jacobson did not designate any students as "nonbloomers" (the equivalent of maze-dull rats), teachers in real life designate such students in this way every day. It is little wonder, then, that some students (i.e., bloomers) live up to our expectations and other students (i.e., nonbloomers) live down to our expectations.

Although research on teacher expectancy conducted since Rosenthal and Jacobson's influential study, which itself has been criticized for major research design flaws (Claiborn, 1969; Elashoff & Snow, 1971; Fleming & Anttonen, 1971; Jensen, 1969; Snow, 1969; Thorndike, 1968), does not always produce the expected performance differences in students (Mendels & Flanders, 1973; Jussim, 1989, 1990), "the effect is observed often enough that its importance should not be discounted" (Smith & Luginbuhl, 1976, p. 265).

**Figure 1.1**
**Same Student, Two Different Teacher Interpretations**

Using the journal *Educational Researcher* as a forum, Wineburg (1987b, pp. 28–37), in an article titled "The Self-Fulfillment of the Self-Fulfilling Prophecy," challenges Rosenthal's research findings. Rosenthal's rebuttal (1987, p. 37–41) follows in an article titled "Pygmalion Effects: Existence, Magnitude, and Social Importance." Finally, Wineburg (1987a, pp. 42–44) provides a rejoinder to Rosenthal's reply in an article titled "Does Research Count in the Lives of Behavioral Scientists?"

Babad (1985) supports Rosenthal's conclusions when she emphatically states, "Expectancy bias is now an undisputed phenomenon" (p. 175). Most teachers recognize (Figure 1.1) that holding high or low expectations, and then acting on those expectations, can create a self-fulfilling prophecy (West & Anderson, 1976; Willis, 1991). Cooper and Tom (1984) conclude "that the existence of expectation effects is well-established" (p. 79).

What appears to be an almost universal need to form expectations about others based upon even the scantiest information may be nature's way of protecting itself. To the extent that a person can see into the future—that is, what may be waiting around the next street corner, what obstacles lie just down the road, or what behavior so-and-so is likely to do next—to that extent this person has a survival advantage over those who cannot see into the future. So, perhaps even inaccurate expectations about the future (often the case when based upon scanty evidence) are better than no expectations whatsoever. Psychologically, at least, one might feel better prepared to face what may come next in life by thinking that you can predict it somewhat.

## DEFINITIONS OF THE SELF-FULFILLING PROPHECY/PYGMALION EFFECT

A review of the literature reveals that many journal articles, doctoral dissertations, books and chapters have been written on the subject of the self-fulfilling prophecy (SFP) or the Pygmalion effect since Rosenthal and Jacobson's mid-1960s research. In spite of this wide and scholarly exposure, most educators do not know enough about the SFP to use it as a conscious and purposeful teaching tool or to recognize when the SFP is being misused to their students' detriment.

First of all, in order to understand and systematically apply the SFP or the Pygmalion effect, one needs to know what the term means. In other words, educators must possess a working definition, preferably a widely shared definition, for the term "self-fulfilling prophecy." What follows are a series of definitions of the SFP or Pygmalion effect, some short and to the point, and some a bit lengthy. Pay attention to what is common among these definitions.

"Expectations about behavior that evoke a situation in which the expectations are confirmed" (Bootzin, Bower, Zajonc, and Hall 1986, p. 628).

"The process by which one's expectations about a person eventually lead that person to behave in ways that confirm those expectations" (Brehm and Kassin 1966, p. 111).

"The notion that the expectation of an event can make it happen; it starts with a false belief which causes new behavior; thus, making the false belief become a true positive reality" (Campbell and Simpson 1992, p. 38).

The SFP "suggests that the quality of interactions between a teacher and a highly regarded pupil differs from the quality of interactions that a less regarded pupil experiences and that this difference is responsible, in part, for the transmission of differential expectations and the expectancy effect" (Firestone and Brody 1975, p. 544).

"The process by which someone's expectations about a person or group leads to the fulfillment of those expectations" (Franzoi 1996, p. 560).

Teacher expectations are "inferences that teachers make of the future behavior or academic achievement of their students, based on what they know about these students now" (Good 1987, p. 132).

"The tendency to confirm our expectations of people by behaving toward them in ways that provoke them to act consistently with those expectations" (Horowitz and Bordens 1995, p. G-6).

The Pygmalion effect, or self-fulfilling prophecy, "causes people to meet the expectations of others" (Loftus 1995, p. 32).

"The self-fulfilling prophecy is, in the beginning, a false definition of the situation evoking a new behavior which makes the originally false conception come true. The specious validity of the self-fulfilling prophecy perpetuates a reign of error. For the prophet will cite the actual course of events as proof that he was right from the very beginning" (Merton 1948, p. 195).

"People's social expectations lead them to act in ways that cause others to confirm their expectations" (Myers 1996, p. 116).

"The literature suggests that self-fulfilling prophecies are often mediated by expectancy-revealing perceiver expressive behaviors; behaviors that suggest to a target how a perceiver feels about him or her. Such expressions may be communicated both nonverbally and verbally, either intentionally or not. Importantly, expectancies influence such expressive behaviors, and these behaviors influence the actions of others" (Neuberg, Judice, Virdin, and Carrillo 1993, p. 410).

The Pygmalion effect is getting people to recognize, believe in, and act on their abilities (Oechsli 1994).

The Pygmalion Effect is a type of self-fulfilling prophecy in which increasing a leader's expectations of subordinates' performance actually improves that performance (Rheem 1995).

"A recurring doctrine in educational psychology is that teacher's attitudes toward an individual child, and more specifically, preconceived expectations of the child's scholastic potential and behaviour, may significantly influence the child's actual performance" (Shaw and Humphreys 1982, p. 313).

"The process by which one person's expectations about another become reality by eliciting behaviors that confirm the expectations" (Smith and Mackie 1995, p. 103).

## THE HALO EFFECT

The halo effect needs to be distinguished from the self-fulfilling effect (Monk, 1983). In the halo effect, one person (i.e., a boyfriend, parent) places a sort of "halo" over another person's head (i.e., girlfriend, child), and through his or her eyes and rose-colored glasses, this person can do no wrong. A neutral observer may wonder why the starry-eyed boyfriend cannot see all that is wrong with his girlfriend or why the parent cannot see the faults of his or her child. To everyone else, the flaws are quite evident. Clearly this is an example of beauty being in the eye of the beholder. The person who has imposed the halo sees (perceives) only what he wants to see, not what actually exists.

For a school-related example of the halo effect, we might have the all-too-common situation where a school calls a student's parents to inform them of the child's disruptive behavior, only to have the parents proclaim, "You must be mistaken, our child would never do something like that. He is such a well-behaved child." What the parents see is colored by the halo they have placed over their child's head. What the parents perceive influences their viewpoint.

Evaluator perceptions, then, not evidence, dictates the evaluation. When perceptions differ from reality, the perceptions win out and, according to Kolb and Jussim (1994), a perceptual bias exists. In classrooms, teachers perceive and then go on to evaluate their students' behaviors and performance in ways that are consistent with their sometimes faulty beliefs. Instead of beauty being in the eye of the beholder, although that too exists in schools, we have the student's behavior and achievement being in the eye of the beholder—the teacher.

When it comes to evaluating student behavior and achievement, the halo effect or perceptual bias has teachers evaluating learners according to how they perceive the students to perform—not how the students actually perform. Thus, high-expectations students can do little or no wrong in both behavior and achievement. These students' responses commonly are evaluated higher than they actually are. Low-expectations students can do little or no right in both behavior and achievement. Students pegged as disruptive or as low achievers are likely to have their performance downgraded in the eye of the evaluator.

When a student's actual performance (behavior or achievement) disagrees with the perception the teacher holds of that student's ability, one of two things must occur to resolve the discrepancy. One, the teacher could admit that he or she has been holding erroneous beliefs regarding the student's abilities. To admit this, though, is to admit that, all along, one's professional judgment has been wrong. Two, the teacher, probably unknowingly, could evaluate the student's performance higher or lower to fit the teacher's own perceptual bias. Too often, the latter method of resolving the discrepancy is selected. Good students' performance continues to be judged good even if it isn't, and poor students' performance continues to be judged poor even if it isn't.

It should be noted that in some cases, the halo effect can serve as the expectations that trigger the start of the self-fulfilling prophecy. In other words, if you see good in someone that isn't actually there, and you are persistent in seeing this good, the person on whom you have placed the halo may just live up to the goodness that you see.

# CHAPTER 2

# MECHANISMS OF THE SELF-FULFILLING PROPHECY

## INTRODUCTION

The self-fulfilling prophecy (SFP) is not simply wishing something were so and, magically, it is so. If this were the case, my mother-in-law would have won the state lottery a long time ago, and I would own a green classic British racing Jaguar-XKE convertible in showroom condition. Both my mother-in-law and I have wished—in fact, have longed—to win the lottery and to own the XKE for decades. She still has not won the big pot in the state lottery, and I still do not own an XKE. I am here to tell you that wishing alone does not make it so!

Although expectations are important, "what a teacher expects matters less for a child's achievement than what a teacher does" (Goldenberg, 1992, p. 522). In other words, the self-fulfilling prophecy is more than a wish or expectation; it is a process composed of a series of steps. Yes, the SFP does begin with the step of making a wish or forming an expectation, and it does end often with the step of the fulfillment of that wish or expectation. But in between this beginning step and this ending step lie a series of other steps. As a process made up of a series of steps, the SFP lends itself to conscious intervention.

After people (i.e., parents, teachers, managers) are informed that the SFP is a process, and after they subsequently are informed about each of the steps in the SFP process, they are in a better position to exercise conscious and purposeful control over the process. That is the goal of this book. Informed people can use their newfound knowledge to heighten the positive effects and lessen the negative effects of the self-fulfilling prophecy. Nowhere is this more important than in the classroom.

## STEPS IN THE SELF-FULFILLING PROPHECY

Good and Brophy (1978) present a five-step model to explain how a teacher's expectations for students often can lead, via differential behaviors, to the fulfillment of these expectations. Each step will be presented and then explained.

Step 1:   Teacher Forms Expectations
Step 2:   Based Upon These Expectations, the Teacher Acts in a Differential Manner
Step 3:   The Teacher's Treatment Tells Each Student What Behavior and Achievement the Teacher Expects
Step 4:   If This Treatment Is Consistent Over Time, and if the Student Does Not Actively Resist, It Will Tend to Shape His or Her Behavior and Achievement
Step 5:   With Time, the Student's Behavior and Achievement Will Conform More Closely to That Expected of Him or Her

### Step 1: Teacher Forms Expectations

On what bases do teachers form expectations?  Like other people, teachers can and do form expectations on anything and everything that they see, feel, touch, smell, or hear.  You could take pen to paper and write from now until the turn of the century those things that can possibly trigger expectations, and you would not need to duplicate any entries.  It would be easier, in fact, to list those things about people that are not capable of triggering expectations.  Your paper would be blank!

For instance, let's examine a common human characteristic—hair—and its power to trigger expectations.  Whether it be people with bushy eyebrows or people with plucked eyebrows, people with straight hair or people with curly hair, people with red hair or people with blond hair, people who part their hair or people who do not part their hair, people with hair or people without hair, someone, somewhere, is using this characteristic to form expectations.

How ridiculous can the basis for our expectations get?  Very ridiculous!  It should not be surprising, in fact, to find that beach-goers form expectations about other beach-goers on something so silly as who has "innee" belly buttons and who has "outee" belly buttons.  Really!  Or take prospective candidates for a university faculty teaching position who are judged more positively if they drink cappuccino coffee than if they don't.  How about people who leave their fresh, hot, french fries to eat last (getting cold and soggy in the meantime) while they eat the rest of their meal?  Or what about people who, when dressing, put on one sock and one shoe and then another sock and another shoe instead of doing it the normal way—putting both socks on first and then putting on both shoes?  Years ago, in an "All in the Family" television program, Archie Bunker went bananas when he saw his new son-in-law, Michael Spivik, putting his shoes and socks on in just such a "strange" manner.  The bottom line is that every human characteristic or observed behavior is capable of triggering an expectation.  Kind of scary, isn't it?

Perhaps the word "triggering," as in the trigger of a gun, is a good word to use when discussing expectations. With a gun, once the trigger is pulled, things happen, and they happen fast—there is almost no stopping them. The trigger triggers a response. Sometimes good things happen—a rabid animal is shot and destroyed, keeping children in the community safe. Sometimes bad things happen—a drive-by shooting kills an innocent citizen. Once expectations are formed, they too trigger a response—sometimes good, sometimes bad.

The exercise in chapter 1 pointed out only too clearly just some of the human characteristics (i.e., weight, ethnic origin) and human situations (i.e., using food stamps at a grocery store) that are capable of triggering expectations. In schools, the target population for this book, "one important factor that places certain groups of children at risk is the operation of differential and very low expectations for what they can accomplish" (Weinstein et al., 1991). Chapters 4 through 13 review the literature regarding how people (often teachers) are inclined to form expectations based on still other human characteristics and human situations.

Before we go on, stop for a moment and think about your own life. Who in your life has had high expectations of you—teachers, parents, employers, mentors, spouse? More than likely, you have lived up to—sometimes down to—the expectations these Pygmalions have held for you. How would your life possibly have been different if you had not had these Pygmalions? Right now, who are Pygmalions for you? Who are you a Pygmalion for?

The term "expectations" is crucial to the triggering of the self-fulfilling prophecy. Just because a person does not use the specific word "expectations" does not mean that subsequent, often damaging, effects do not occur. Once expectations are formed, the "self-fulfilling prophecies and expectancy confirmation sequences may thus begin to operate before disconfirming information is available, ensuring the perpetuation of stereotypes" (Deaux & Lewis, 1984, p. 1003). What happens is that as soon as expectations are formed, we tend to search the present as well as the past for confirming information. Come hell or high water, what we believe (expect) to be true is going to become true—even if we have to go so far as to create confirming information that does not exist. People who form expectations have a personal stake in having them become confirmed!

### Step 2: Based Upon These Expectations, the Teacher Acts in a Differential Manner

*Conveying Expectations: A Four-Factor Theory*

Different expectations can lead to different treatments. When they do, the self-fulfilling prophecy is off and running. This cause-and-effect connection between an expectation and a subsequent treatment is the basis for the second step in the self-fulfilling prophecy process—differential behaviors.

How does one person convey his or her expectations to another person? These factors constitute the repertoire of behaviors available to teachers. There must be factors of some sort being used to convey expectations; otherwise, the self-fulfilling prophecy would reduce simply to "wish it (expect it), and it would be so." A prerequisite to exerting some conscious control over the self-fulfilling prophecy is knowing and understanding what these conveying-of-expectancies factors are.

The conveying-of-expectancies factors identified by Rosenthal (1973a, 1973b, 1974) in his Four-Factor Theory, and regularly cited by others (e.g., Loftus, 1992), are *climate*, *feedback*, *input*, and *output*. These factors act as "expectancy-revealing perceiver expressive behaviors: behaviors that suggest to the target how the perceiver feels about him or her" (Neuberg, Judice, Virdin, & Carrillo, 1993, p. 410).

*Factor one—climate.* Climate refers to the socioemotional mood or spirit, often communicated nonverbally (e.g., smiling and nodding more often, providing greater eye contact, or a more direct eye gaze, leaning closer to the student), created by the person holding the expectation (Chaikin, Sigler, & Derlega, 1974; Rosenthal & DePaulo, 1979). One could describe the climate for high-expectations students as being positive and the climate for low-expectations students as being negative.

Most human beings, including children, are able to decode the climate quickly and accurately. Students know almost instantly whether or not they are in a positive climate, one that is warm, caring, supportive, and encouraging. They know equally quickly when they find themselves in a negative climate. Students want to stay in the former climate; they want to escape the latter climate—mentally or physically.

What compounds the situation is that when students find themselves in a positive climate, they emit their own nonverbal signals that help to create a positive climate, in return, for the expectations holder. Thus, the original expectations holder (i.e., teacher) can feel that the students want to remain in his or her company and responds accordingly. Each person helps to create a mutually satisfying positive climate for the other.

On the contrary, when students find themselves in a negative climate, they send nonverbal signals telling the original expectations holder (i.e., teacher) that they would prefer to be almost anywhere else but in the teacher's company. In return, when the teacher senses the students' negative climate, the teacher may translate his or her feeling into a belief that the students do not care about the assignment in question or the course in general. The teacher now has "evidence" that his or her original low expectations of the students were justified! Once again, the teacher responds accordingly—this time to the mutual disadvantage of teacher and students.

Ask yourself when and where (not if) you have created positive or negative climates for different students. Why? Did it have something to do with the expectations (high or low) that you held for these students? Recall situations when it was obvious that teachers created positive or negative climates for you.

Could you tell?  How could you tell?  Why do you suppose these teachers created the climate they did for your?  In hindsight, did it have something to do with the expectations they held for you?  Clearly, teacher expectations are a crucial element of the educational climate; they can influence students' motivation, behavior, and achievement (Arganbright, 1983).

*Factor two—feedback.*  Feedback refers to providing both affective and cognitive responses to students.  Differential affective responses include providing more praise and less criticism for high-expectations students than for low-expectations students (Cooper & Tom, 1984).  Differential cognitive responses include more, and more detailed, as well as higher-quality feedback as to the correctness of a response and more evidence that a response is leading to some overall goal for high-expectations students than for low-expectations students.  This feedback can be delivered either in a one-to-one format or via abundant comments inserted in written assignments.

Ask yourself when the amount of affective and/or cognitive feedback provided to a student varied due to the expectations you held of that student.  Have you caught yourself writing lots and lots of comments—complete sentences—on higher-expectations students' papers and writing fewer, as well as shorter, comments on lower-expectations students' papers?  Have you caught yourself thinking, "why bother writing many comments on some of the lower expectations students' papers—they will not read (or follow) anyhow?"

When going over a student's work in your office, have you caught yourself verbally providing more feedback to some students than to others?  If so, what was different about these students?  Did they differ in the expectations that you held for them?

*Factor three—input.*  Input translates into the fact that teachers tend to teach more to students of whom they expect more (Rosenthal, 1973a).  This differential treatment can be observed whether teachers are teaching a classroom full of students or responding to students on a one-to-one basis.

Personally, I sometimes catch myself responding differently to different students who come to my office to discuss a project or term paper.  For students for whom I hold high expectations, I take this opportunity to teach them more during our one-to-one meetings.  For instance, I am likely to introduce and explain the workings of the Educational Resources Information System (ERIC, a CD-ROM-based searching system) to high-expectations students whom I see struggling with their review of the literature.  I may even walk them down to the library—just down the hall—and actually show them how to use the ERIC system.

I devote this extra time and energy to these high-expectations students because I believe (expect) that they will actually make use of, as well as appreciate, what I teach them.  To be honest, I don't always have the same expectations for low-expectations students and, as a result, I spend less time and effort teaching them additional information or skills during their scheduled meetings with me.

I might rationalize that there is not enough time and energy in any one day to meet all students' needs, and therefore my time and energy must be rationed. These precious resources must go to the most deserving students—the high-expectations students. Yet we know that differential treatment of students, conscious or unconscious, can lead to a self-fulfilling prophecy (Didham, 1990). Does treating high-expectations and low-expectations students differently make me a terrible teacher? Not necessarily. What would make me a terrible teacher would be if, once I realized that I was shortchanging low-expectations students, I knowingly and purposefully continued this differential treatment.

*Factor four—output.*   Factor four, output, is where teachers encourage, through their verbal and nonverbal behaviors, greater responsiveness from those students from whom they expect more.   These behaviors provide high-expectations students with greater opportunities to question, to seek clarification, and to ask for further explanation. Further, high-expectations students are called on more often, asked more difficult questions, given more time to respond, and prompted or cued in order to correct their partially correct answers (Loftus, 1992; Rosenthal, 1973a).

Continuing my personal example of when students come in to my office for a one-to-one meeting regarding a term paper or project, I find that I regularly ask high-expectations students if they have any questions, if I need to clarify or further explain something I've said, or, in general, if I can be of help. I catch myself dismissing lower-expectations students with verbal or nonverbal messages that seem to say, "That's it; it is time for you to leave."

With respect to making greater overall demands of high-expectations students, I catch myself saving the easier, often recall-type questions for the low-expectations students. The nature of these basically right or wrong, low-level questions is such that if they are answered correctly, little recognition is deserved (or provided), and if they are answered incorrectly, little prompting or cueing can be given to improve the quality of the response.

The more challenging, often application-type and analysis-type questions are reserved for the high-expectations students. I must admit that I also work more with high-expectations students' answers in order to get the higher quality responses that I know (believe) they are capable of providing. High-expectations students, and the responses they generate to my more difficult questions, in effect, become colleagues or coteachers in helping me teach what I want to teach. Once again, does my differential treatment (i.e., output) suggest that I am a terrible teacher? The answer is no if, once I recognize my differential treatment of output, I take corrective measures.

*Conveying-of-Expectations Behaviors*

There are some specific differential behaviors that teachers and others regularly use to convey their expectations. A number of these conveying-of-expectations teacher behaviors (Brophy, 1985) are listed below, each with an accompanying example. Several of these examples are from a often-cited article by Rist (1970) titled "Student Social Class and Teacher Expectations: The Self-Fulfilling Prophecy in Ghetto Education," published in the *Harvard Educational Review*.

This article describes Rist's observation of the criteria an urban kindergarten teacher appeared to use in order to seat her students at three tables (Tables 1, 2, and 3), and then records the teacher's interactions with these students throughout the school year. Once table placement was assigned, a sort of caste system developed whereby it was almost impossible for a child's placement to be changed (Dusek, 1975). The article ends by summarizing the Table 3, low-expectations children's achievement and behaviors at the end of the year.

For other examples of these conveying-of-expectations teacher behaviors, instances reported by education majors who have participated in semester-long, in-the-schools, field experiences are used. Still other examples of these conveying-of-expectations teacher behaviors will be drawn from the author's own observations.

*Differential treatment: Low- and high-expectations students*

• Seating low-expectations students farthest from the teacher and/or seating them all together in a group are some ways teachers convey their expectations. Students soon learn to decode the equivalent of the red birds, blue birds, and yellow birds—high-expectations, medium-expectations, low-expectations students, respectively, for example.

Rist's study describes how, by the eighth day of school, an urban kindergarten teacher had formed her permanent seating arrangement and placed her "ideal" students—those who most often were well dressed, spoke Standard American English, and were from families with higher levels of education where both parents worked—at Table 1 which was physically closest to her. In effect, these children looked and acted a lot like the teacher herself. Table 1 students were the high-expectations students.

By contrast, the students at Table 3, physically farthest from the teacher, most often were poorly dressed, carried a smell of urine, had matted or unprocessed hair, were from families on welfare, and responded to the teacher using a black dialect. The low-expectations students at Table 3 definitely did not look, smell, act, or talk like the teacher.

• Praising low-expectations students more frequently and more excessively than high-expectations students for marginal or inadequate responses provides signals to students.

A college student named Susan recounts her own elementary school experience where, week after week, she failed to get a perfect spelling paper and thus never earned the coveted gold star on her paper. Finally, through exhaustive study, Susan got all of her weekly spelling words correct. Her reward? The teacher announced to the class, "Look, everyone, Susan finally got all of her spelling words correct. We are going to give her not one, but two gold stars."

Another college student describes his field-experience teacher's treatment of low-expectations students. "When Larry, an academically slower student, answers even the simplest of questions, Mrs. X heaps on the praise. Larry and all of the other children know that his response did not deserve that much praise. I feel sorry for Larry; his face turns so red!"

• Teachers can convey what they expect by giving low-expectations students the answer; waiting less time for "lows" to answer; offering lows fewer clues, prompts, or hints; and restating the original question less often for lows than for high-expectations students.

Perhaps out of a pedagogical guilty conscience, recognizing that one *should* involve all students in class discussion, teachers do call on low-expectations students. Unfortunately, when a low-expectations student hesitates before answering, perhaps to compose his or her thoughts, this pause is interpreted by the teacher as "evidence" that the student does not know the answer.

For high-expectations students, the teacher knows that the child knows the answer. Any hesitation before answering is interpreted as conscious deliberation, wisely weighing his or her words before responding—a characteristic of a good student. Consequently, precious time is allotted for the student to respond, constructive hints are delivered (e.g., "Now, Sam, you remember our discussion yesterday about"), supportive statements are offered (e.g., "Come on, Carol, I know that you know the answer"), and partially correct responses are accepted and then expanded upon by the teacher to make them correct (e.g., "Well, Joe, that's the general idea. To be more specific").

• Paying less attention to low-expectations students than to high-expectations students in academic situations (e.g., smiling and nodding less often, and maintaining less eye contact) is another way teachers differentiate between students.

Rist's study reports that as the school year progressed, the urban kindergarten teacher under study paid less and less attention to the low-expectations students sitting at Table 3, the table physically farthest from her. In fact, during a one-hour period late in the school year, not a single act of teacher communication was directed toward any child at Table 3 except for two commands for the children to "sit down." Even more telling is the fact that as the year progressed, the attempts by the Table 3 children themselves to elicit the attention of the teacher were much fewer than they were earlier in the school year.

• Teachers sometimes provide low-expectations students with less feedback and with less-accurate and less-detailed feedback than that provided to high-expectations students.

Midterm papers are collected, stacked to the ceiling in the professor's office, and ready for the labor-intensive process of being read and graded. As the professor reads the papers, grammatical errors are targeted, spelling mistakes are circled, marginal comments are jotted down, and evaluative summary comments are composed.

Consistent with Rosenthal's (1974) Four-Factor Theory, the amount and quality of instructor-provided feedback will vary with the expectations the teacher holds for each student. High-expectations students will receive more and higher-quality feedback than will low-expectations students.

Consciously or unconsciously, many busy instructors, believing that they have to allocate their precious resources of time and energy, may feel that it is relatively useless to provide extensive feedback to low-expectations students. After all, low-expectations students either will not take the time to read and digest the feedback or, if they do, it will have little impact on their future performance. Not so for high-expectations students. Hence, the high-expectations student, like the first-hatched chick in a brood in nature, gets all the nourishment—worms for the first-hatched stronger chick; positive and supportive feedback for the high-expectations student.

• Some teachers wait less time for low-expectations students to answer questions and then quickly ask a high-expectations student to help out by giving the correct answer, interrupting the performance of low-expectations students more frequently than that of high-expectations students (e.g., Allington, 1980).

As a skit, the kindergarten teacher in Rist's study had the students act out the roles of mother, father, and two children eating supper at the dining room table and sharing what each had done during the day. When Sam, a Table 2 child (who in real life had no father) stumbled in his response while playing the role of the son, instead of providing time for him to compose his answer, the teacher immediately asked Milt, a high-expectations Table 1 child to take Sam's place and show him how the role should be played. Of note is the fact that no low-expectations Table 3 students were asked to participate.

• Criticizing low-expectations students more frequently than high-expectations students for incorrect public responses and praising low-expectations students less frequently than high-expectations students for successful public responses are still other differential teacher behaviors (e.g., Babad, Inbar, & Rosenthal, 1982).

Although this seems incredulous, research supports this all-too-common teacher behavior. One would think that low-expectations students could profit from being criticized less and praised even more than their high-expectations student peers. One wonders why teachers would do just the opposite!

• Finally, some teachers may call on, or in other ways initiate contacts with, low-expectations students less often than high-expectations students to answer classroom questions or to make public presentations before the class (e.g., Firestone & Brody, 1975; Given, 1974; Smey-Richman, 1989).

Rist's study reports that two months into the school year, the teacher told the class that they could take turns sharing their Halloween experiences with classmates. When the time came for making their public demonstration, no children from Table 3, the low-expectations table, were invited to share their experiences. One child from Table 2 and five children from Table 1, the high-expectations children sitting closest to the teacher, were asked to share their experiences.

*Summary*

Research findings (Good, 1982, 1984; Research for Better Schools, 1987; Rosenthal, 1989) clearly demonstrate that teachers' attitudes (i.e., expectations) and subsequent behaviors (i.e., as in Rosenthal's Four-Factor Theory) have significant effects upon student achievement. After examining the results of 345 studies of interpersonal self-fulfilling prophecies, Rosenthal and Rubin (1978) conclude that "the reality of the phenomenon is beyond doubt and the mean size of the effect is clearly not trivial" (p. 385).

### Step 3: The Teacher's Treatment Tells Each Student What Behavior and Achievement the Teacher Expects

Human beings of all ages, including children, are uncanny at being able to tell what others think they are capable of doing and/or achieving (Weinstein, Marshall, Sharp, & Botkin, 1987). Students acquire information about their abilities by observing their teachers' differential treatment of high and low achievers (Brattesani, Weinstein, & Marshall, 1984). No matter what the source of information, whether it be verbal and/or nonverbal, the fact is that most of us are capable of deciphering what it is that others expect from us. Once we get the message, we then revise our own expectations up or down to coincide with those delivered to us by important people in our lives—parents, teachers, friends.

The Four-Factor Theory (i.e., climate, feedback, input, and output) described in the previous section provides multiple ways for the expectations messages to be delivered and recognized. Sometimes the expectations messages are subtle and perhaps open to interpretation. Other times the expectations messages are loud and clear and may as well be screamed!

### Step 4: If This Treatment Is Consistent Over Time, and if the Student Does Not Actively Resist, It Will Tend to Shape His or Her Behavior and Achievement

Before expectations can affect pupil performance, they must be associated with consistently differential teacher behaviors toward pupils so that these behaviors elicit stable changes in the pupils' behavior (Moore, 1984). A lot of who you are, or at least who most children are, is determined, in part, by what others tell you that you are over a period of time. If children, in effect, are relatively blank slates when they are born, these slates are filled, a little bit at a time, with evaluations (i.e., expectations) made by, among others, parents and teachers.  If a consistent string of teacher-delivered evaluations fills a student's slate, then the odds are that soon he or she will begin to believe those expectations.   Why not?   In the absence of conflicting evaluations (i.e., expectations), the student's behavior and achievement will be shaped.

Early-childhood and elementary-age children (and minority children) are most at risk in believing teachers' consistently delivered evaluations.   This is especially true in self-contained classrooms where a single teacher is in a position to play a major role in influencing how a number of children feel about themselves and their abilities.  One hundred eight days of school is a long time to hear the same evaluative messages regarding what a teacher thinks of you. You would have to be very strong or have other sources of valued evaluations not to be affected by what a teacher thinks that you are capable of achieving. Pity the child who receives consistently negative evaluations.  Some children who "do not play the good student role and score towards the lower end of the continuum [academic] may be among those particularly vulnerable to negative spirals" (Smead, 1984, p. 154) caused, in part, by teachers' negative expectations.

### Step 5: With Time, the Student's Behavior and Achievement Will Conform More Closely to That Expected of Him or Her

Referring once again to Rist's (1970) study titled "Student Social Class and Teacher Expectations: The Self-Fulfilling Prophecy in Ghetto Education," the impact of treating the high expectations, Table 1 students one way and the low-expectations, Table 3 students another way is revealed in the kindergarten teacher's end-of-year comments on the children.

Of the Table 1 students, the teacher says, "Those at Table 1 consistently gave the most responses throughout the year and seemed most interested and aware of what was going on in the classroom."  Of the Table 2 and Table 3 students, the teacher says:

It seems to me that some of the children at Table 2 and most of the children at 3 at times seem to have no idea of what is going on in the classroom and were off in another world by themselves. (Ironically, the teacher physically placed them "off in another world.") It just appears that some can do it and some cannot.  I don't think that it is the teaching that affects those that cannot do it, but some are just basically low achievers.

# THE SELF-FULFILLING PROPHECY IN ACTION

## A Dissertation Proposal—Almost an SFP Nightmare!

When I was in graduate school, I had a friend who was trying to select a topic for what he hoped would be the focus of his doctoral dissertation. Now, what should he investigate? Given that he had had experience as a student-teaching supervisor and that he considered himself to be a good judge of character, he proposed to investigate whether or not a seasoned student-teaching supervisor (such as himself) could predict, with greater than chance accuracy, whether student teachers (such as those he would supervise) would or would not excel in the classroom. He offered just such a dissertation proposal to his doctoral committee. They, of course, turned him down.

Had my fellow graduate student been familiar with the self-fulfilling prophecy and its five-step mechanism, he never would have proposed this design in the first place. Recall the five steps in the SFP mechanism outlined above. His faulty research design would have included the first step in the SFP process, forming expectations ahead of time about which students he believed would or would not excel by the end of the student-teaching semester. On what student-teacher characteristics was he going to base his initial prediction of success versus failure? This was always a mystery to me. The point is, he was going to do the first step in the SFP process—he was going to form expectations.

Given that he himself was going to be assigned as the student teachers' university supervisor, there is little doubt, according to self-fulfilling prophecy theory, that he would have done the second step in the SFP process. He certainly would have been inclined to treat high-expectations student teachers one way and low-expectations student teachers another way—i.e., practice differential behaviors. These differential behaviors would have occurred even if the supervisor were not aware that he was doing this.

Step three of the SFP would have occurred because his differential treatment of the student teachers would have been sensed by them. They would have sensed, through the supervisor's verbal and nonverbal behaviors, exactly what behaviors and levels of achievement he expected from each of them. Step four of the SFP would have occurred throughout the semester, when, through supervisor observation after supervisor observation, consistent differential treatment would have been sensed. Step four, in effect, is a continually occurring step three. Of importance to step four is the fact that student teachers would normally be observed by only one student-teaching supervisor. Further, the student teacher's supervisor, and not the student teacher's cooperating teacher, assigned the final grade for student teaching. Thus, the supervisor's evaluation was the evaluation—the one that counted!

Step five of the SFP process would have been realized by the end of the semester when—surprise, surprise—high-expectations student teachers turned out to be successful and low-expectations student teachers turned out to be unsuccessful!

**Figure 2.1**
**"Teaching" to Locker Numbers**

**A Second-Grade Teacher's Bright Idea—Almost Another SFP Disaster**

As the story goes, there was this second-grade teacher, Miss New Teacher, who at the very beginning of the school year was standing in the principal's office requesting additional supplies for several unexpected student additions to her classroom. Just as she was making her request, the principal's secretary screamed, "Mr. Tomaino, we need you out here right away!" The principal ran to the outer office to respond to the emergency, leaving Miss New Teacher standing next to his desk. While waiting, Miss New Teacher glanced around and noticed her class roster sitting on Mr. Tomaino's desk. Next to each student's name was a number: David = 131, Carol = 93, Joseph = 89, Rebecca = 111, and so forth. Miss New Teacher hurriedly jotted down the names and IQs.

Throughout the school year, Miss New Teacher repeatedly would refer to these student IQs as she asked questions, assigned tasks, and generally interacted with students. Her goal was to challenge each student to the limits of his or her IQ. At the end of the school year, all of the teachers were having a final meeting with Mr. Tomaino. At this meeting, Mr. Tomaino asked if there were any suggestions for making the next school year an even better one than the year that had just ended.

Sheepishly, Miss New Teacher raised her hand. She said, "I think that you should provide all teachers with lists of the students' IQs. I found that having these IQs really helped me in my teaching this year. I was able to challenge students with high IQs and ended up getting a lot out of them—they really excelled. At the same time, I made sure not to overwhelm the less bright students with challenges too great for them."

Mr. Tomaino responded, "How did you get the students' IQs?" Miss New Teacher said, with her face turning a little bit red, "I saw them on your desk that first day of school and jotted them down." Mr. Tomaino responded in horror that those were not the students' IQs; they were the students' locker numbers! She had been teaching to the students' locker numbers (Figure 2.1) the entire year. And, sure enough, students had lived up to—or down to—their respective locker numbers.

## CONCLUSION

What the self-fulfilling prophecy process does is label someone and then have that person treated as if that label were correct. Over time, a hastily assigned label may become an accurate description of this person. A recent article in a university newspaper, *The Daily Collegian*, by Oakes (1996), captures the gist of the SFP process and the damage that it can do. Oakes says that people like the fact that buildings and streets around them are labeled. It gives them a sense of security. "Unfortunately, many of us seek the same security when we look at people" (p. 11). Once we label a person, "it shapes our view of the person. It affects how we act and react toward the person. Labels are easy. We don't have to get to know the person.  We can just assume what the person is like.  Labeling deprives you of the most fulfilling relationships" (p. 11).

# CHAPTER 3

# THE SFP: A GLOBAL PERSPECTIVE

## INTRODUCTION

The self-fulfilling prophecy is a worldwide phenomenon. Researching the SFP in other countries finds that their teachers, too, are treating students differently according to the expectations the teachers have of them (e.g., based on students' race, ethnicity, and gender). Selected examples of the SFP are presented in this chapter. Perhaps we can learn a thing or two from this sampling of international SFP research.

## SELECTED SFP RESEARCH FROM ACROSS THE WORLD

### Great Britain

Crano and Mellon (1978) investigated teacher expectations of over 4,000 British primary school students and reported that a cause-and-effect relationship existed between teacher expectations and children's achievements. In addition to expectations for academic performance, teachers held expectations for students' social performance (i.e., work habits, pleasantness in class, attitude towards work). This latter source of expectations, social performance, produced the more consistent results.

A University of Wales study by Butler-Por (1989) was designed to develop and evaluate a new treatment for academic underachievement. The subjects were 36 underachievers of gifted and average ability and their 12 classroom teachers. The treatment consisted of using the steps outlined in Glasser's *Reality Therapy* (1965). Among the results, it was found that teacher expectations were closely related to the success of the treatment.

Kenealy, Frude, and Shaw (1988) rated the physical attractiveness of one thousand 11- to 12-year-old children and then measured the degree to which teachers associated the children's physical attractiveness with selected academic and social traits. The results of the study "show some significant tendencies on the part of teachers to judge attractive children as more sociable, more popular, academically brighter, more confident, and more likely to be leaders than unattractive children" (p. 380). The results were similar for both boys and girls.

Another study in Wales (Shaw & Humphreys, 1982) investigated the influence of children's dentofacial appearance on teachers' expectations. Head teachers in nine secondary schools distributed a 16-item questionnaire, allegedly designed to assess students' academic ability, social relationships, and personality, to a total of 320 teachers. Each questionnaire was accompanied by a standardized educational history school record card and one of several different photographs of attractive and unattractive students. The children's pictures had different dentofacial arrangements—for example, normal incisors, prominent incisors, missing incisors. The results of the study showed that teachers did not show any preferential bias for the attractive children. Yet in an earlier study by Shaw (1981), when these same test photographs were shown to lay adults, they associated normal dental appearance with, among other traits, intelligence and the likelihood of attracting friends.

Teacher expectations and the able child were investigated in a study by Lee-Corbin (1994). In a pilot study, the author interviewed a small number of teachers and students, focusing upon, respectively, their teaching and learning styles. She concluded that there were common elements, the basis for expectation formation, for field dependent (FD) students and for field independent (FI) students and teachers.

On a lighter note, in the novel *Paper Money*, Ken Follett describes an action-packed caper of high finance and underworld villainy that takes place in England. A London newspaper editor, defending why the paper should not print what to that point was still just a rumor, tells his young reporter, "We're going to leave it, and I'm going to tell you why. One: we can't predict the collapse of a bank, because our prediction on its own would be enough to cause that collapse. Just to ask questions about the bank's viability would set the City all a-tremble" (Follett, p. 217).

### Netherlands

Jungbluth's (1994) research found that education in Dutch schools is still ruled indirectly by the principles of social class, whereby educational opportunity for adolescent migrants in the Netherlands is influenced by teacher expectations. The study was carried out in 44 Dutch schools with a high concentration of migrant students.

### India

Sakya (1980) researched 60 middle-caste-level male high school teachers in an effort to determine if students' caste had any effect on the teachers' expectations. Three pairs of essays written by high school students, each pair having one identified by caste, were evaluated by the teachers. The study finds that middle-caste teachers showed high-expectation biases toward high-caste students. Beliefs in the academic superiority of Brahman (high-caste) children appear to be ingrained in the minds of the middle-caste teachers.

### Israel

A study in Israel by Eden (1990a), one of a number of Eden's studies by this author investigating the self-fulfilling prophecy (i.e., Eden, 1984; Eden, 1986; Eden, 1988a, 1988b; Eden & Ravid, 1982; Eden & Shani, 1982), concludes that "managers get the subordinates they expect" (p. 884). It further claimed that "expecting effective performance harnesses the Pygmalion effect and renders the SFP an ally in the unending struggle for increased productivity" (p. 884). In another study in the same region of the world, Dvir, Eden, and Banjo (1995) tested the Pygmalion hypothesis among women in the Israeli Defense Forces. The researchers found that the hypothesis was confirmed among women led by men, but not among women led by women! Although this Israel-based research focuses upon the work environment of manager/employee and the military environment of superior/subordinate, the parallel to classroom world of teacher/student is clear.

Also in Israel, Babad and Taylor (1992) conducted a study that focused exclusively on nonverbal communication. Eighty-five people, ranging from 10-year-olds to experienced high school teachers, acted as judges and viewed Israeli teachers interacting, in Hebrew, with Israeli students. Using only teachers' facial expressions and body language, the judges were able to distinguish between the high- and low-expectancy students. Apparently, expectancy-related behavior is not culture specific and is easily detected, even by 10-year-olds.

In an earlier study, Tal and Babad (1989) tested whether or not Israeli teachers could exert conscious control over their nonverbal emotional messages so that students would be unaware of who were the teachers' favorites (i.e., teachers' pets), a version of high-expectancy students. Apparently the teachers' emotional messages (feelings) were both pervasive and transparent, because the researchers found that students were able to identify teachers' pets with overwhelming consensus.

### New Zealand

In a study of 90 nine-year-olds in five ethnically mixed New Zealand elementary classrooms, results showed that the Maori (Polynesian minority) pupils were perceived less favorably than the Pakeha (white majority) pupils. Negative perceptions and expectations for Polynesian children led to their being treated similarly to others expected to be of low ability and helped to maintain the status quo of lower achievement (St. George, 1983, p. 48). These expectations were in line with the commonly held stereotype that Maoris have lower intellectual and academic ability than their Pakeha counterparts (Vaughan, 1972).

### Australia

Camaren's (1981) study tested the relationship of attractiveness and prosocial attributions among ethnic groups in a multiethnic society (Australia). Three groups of 30 female kindergarten students, representing the dominant (Anglo), near dominant (Italian), and minority (Aboriginal) cultures, were used as raters. Each rater group assigned social attributions to photographs of children where attractiveness and ethnicity were varied. The results revealed that Anglos were more often selected as attractive and accorded high prosocial attributions. Aboriginals were shunned and accorded high antisocial attributions, even by like-ethnic raters.

### Malaysia

In an effort to identify institutional characteristics that could be used to differentiate between effective and ineffective schools, Mohd.Nor (1990) used field research methods (i.e., interviews, observations) to collect data on four Malaysian rural secondary schools. Among the author's identified differentiating characteristics was teacher expectations of students.

### Papua New Guinea

A study by Moore (1984) finds that in six Papua New Guinea community schools and five provincial high schools, teachers favored the more able students. In particular, teachers directed a disproportionately large number of questions, offered more praise, and delivered less disapproval to students judged to be most able. Therefore, a disparity exists in the distribution of these important aspects of the teachers' communication—"in exact concordance with what one would expect from the self-fulfilling prophecy hypothesis" (p. 161).

### South Korea

Robinson's (1994) long-term study in six classrooms in a South Korean elementary school investigated whether or not students' social-economic status (SES) triggers teachers' self-fulfilling prophecies. This work was an outgrowth of the author's earlier research (1983). Robinson reported evidence supporting several hypotheses, including the following: (1) teachers acquire and hold expectations about students from differing SES, (2) teachers operationalize their SES expectations through differential behavior, and (3) differential teacher behaviors affect students' academic performance (1994, p. 506).

## Canada

Bognar (1983) presented 208 teachers and student teachers enrolled in summer school courses at Memorial University (Newfoundland, Canada) with a factitious report card for a Grade 6 student. Each report card had a photograph attached that varied only by gender and attractiveness of the student. Two surprises emerged. One, the author found little in the way of expectation effects based upon the variables of gender and attractiveness. Two, the greater the amount of the teachers' university education, the more negative were the teachers' expectations of the children.

In a cognitive dissonance theory-based study, Bognar (1982) attempted to determine if students' achievement test results would influence teachers' expectations. The study, using 13 Grade 6 teachers and 285 students, showed that teachers' expectations remained intact, in spite of standardized test results that, at times, provided conflicting evidence. "The lack of change in expectations as a result of test feedback raises many disturbing issues about teachers' perceptions of students; the general lack of responsiveness of expectations to discrepant feedback suggests the rigidity of expectations" (p. 186). What chance do students have to improve their position in the eyes of their teachers if these teachers tend to reject evidence that is in conflict with their expectations?

Clifton and Bulcock (1987) investigated whether or not Ontario teachers expect children from some ethnic groups (i.e., French- and Yiddish-speaking students) to learn more and faster than children from other ethnic groups. The authors concluded that "when sex, socioeconomic status, intellectual ability, assigned grades, and academic aspirations are controlled, there are differences between Yiddish and French students. Teachers have higher expectations for the Yiddish students than for the French students" (pp. 308–309).

Rampaul, Singh, and Didyk (1984) investigated the expectations of two teachers (males) of 41 third and fourth grade students in a school in northern Manitoba. The correlations found between academic achievement of students and teacher expectations were significant. Therefore, the authors' hypothesis that there would be a positive relationship between academic achievement and teacher expectations was supported. Recommendations for all prospective and in-service teachers of Native children were offered.

Dion (1973), an often-cited researcher, assessed whether or not Ontario preschoolers would be able to discriminate differences in facial attractiveness among photographs judged by adults to vary in attractiveness. The results indicated that "among young children, facial attractiveness is a discernible social cue which has already begun to acquire evaluative connotations" (pp. 187–188). Attractive children were selected more often as potential friends and judged to exhibit greater positive social behaviors.

In another study with a Canadian audience, Dion (1974) investigated the relationship between children's physical attractiveness and sex as potential elicitors of differential adult punitiveness. The evaluators were approximately 50 white males and females enrolled in an introductory psychology course. "A cross-sex leniency effect occurred which was mediated by a child's attractiveness" (p. 777).

## SUMMARY

It is obvious that the self-fulfilling prophecy has no geographic boundaries. People are people, and the expectations they form, no matter the country, trigger the SFP. The point of this chapter is not so much the exact findings of the research cited, but more the fact that no matter where one looks across the globe, the SFP is deemed worth studying. The widespread use and abuse of the SFP has prompted scholars and practitioners alike to try to better understand the SFP and, one hopes, move ever closer to limiting its negative impacts and magnifying its positive impacts. The world views the self-fulfilling prophecy as a force to be reckoned with.

# PART II

# SFP CATEGORIES

After explaining the difference between manipulated expectations and natural expectations, part II synthesizes the results of expectations research, citing both classic (e.g., Adams, Brophy, Dion, Dusek, Good, Rosenthal), as well as more contemporary studies. The expectations research is divided into observable human categories that are highlighted in chapter 4 through chapter 13. Although these chapters are relatively short, their point is to concentrate the reader's attention on one expectations-focused human feature at a time—for example, gender, race, body build. Chapter 13 looks at how the SFP is used on teachers by students—an eye-opening revelation for some educators.

Rather than simply reporting the volumes of research on the subject of expectations, part 2 is organized by categories, based upon such human characteristics as gender, race, ethnicity, body features, socioeconomic level, and age. The personal testimonials in part 3 will also address one or more of these SFP expectation categories.

Much of the research reported in part 2, especially as one observable human expectation category at a time is the focus of study, may be eye-opening to the reader. Further, much of the research also will be disturbing—perhaps disturbing enough to cause readers to look into their own lives and then, if required, to take corrective actions. Avenues for training-oriented corrective actions for both preservice and in-service teachers are outlined in chapter 14.

Chapters 4 through 13 are organized as follows:

Introduction—Presents a general example or two of the expectation category in question

What the SFP Research Has to Say—Presents a series of research-based studies documenting the effects of the expectation category in question

A Time for Introspection—What are Your Expectations?—Presents an opportunity for readers to stop and to engage in some self-analysis, some soul-searching, regarding their own use (or abuse) of this expectation category

## MANIPULATED VERSUS NATURAL EXPECTATIONS RESEARCH

The expectations research reported in part 2 falls into one of two paradigms—manipulated or natural. Both of these research designs have been used by researchers to establish links between the teacher education variable, expectations, (Figure 3.1) and a variety of pupil performance measures (Dusek & O'Connell, 1973; Hoge, 1984; Smead, 1984).

### Manipulated Expectations

Manipulated expectations research, the more common type, occurs when the experimenter purposely misleads a subject (e.g., graduate student, teacher, employer, colleague) in a study and then observes how this person "acts" on his or her newly provided expectations. These experiments are referred to by Blease (1983) as studies of induced teacher bias, and by Mendels and Flanders (1973) as studies of contrived expectations.

In Rosenthal and Jacobson's classic study, as described in their book *Pygmalion in the Classroom* (1968a), teachers were lied to—they were told that approximately 20% of their students were likely to be intellectual bloomers. Rosenthal and Jacobson then observed the teachers in order to determine if, and in what way, they acted in a differential manner toward the designated bloomers.

This type of research often has the advantage of amplifying the desired results as well as better insuring that the predicted effects will occur when and where the researcher is available to observe and record them. The generalizability, though, of such studies to the real world is suspect.

### Natural Expectations

Natural expectations research, referred to by Blease (1983) as studies of teacher expectancy, takes place when the experimenter does his or her best to fade into the background and simply observe how one subject "naturally" acts toward another subject. Blease refers to these as studies of teacher expectancy. For example, how do teachers who have not been purposely misled with false expectations about students' intellectual prowess act toward these students. Do teachers act in a differential manner? Do they "naturally" treat more intellectually capable students one way and less intellectually capable students another way? Does the gender, race, or socioeconomic status of the student influence teachers' "natural" reactions toward students?

The word "natural" has been placed in quotes in order to call into question whether or not there really are such things as "natural" expectations. To suggest that expectations are natural is to suggest that they are innate, that we were preprogrammed from birth with these expectations, and that's how it is! If instead we accept that infants are born with a blank slate (tabula rasa) regarding what to expect of others, then we also have to accept that these same infants

**Figure 3.1**
**Teacher Sizing Up This Year's Students**

learn the expectations they will hold as they grow older. Hence, maybe there is no such thing as natural expectations; all expectations are learned. But for the sake of classifying the studies reported in part 2 of this book, "natural" expectations research will be that research where the experimenter has made no special effort to color, influence, or sway a subject's previously possessed expectations. According to Mendels and Flanders (1973), natural expectations are more potent determinants of expectations than are manipulated expectations.

# CHAPTER 4

# GENDER AND THE SFP

## INTRODUCTION

Boys will be boys, girls will be girls, and the late French singer Maurice Chevalier applauds the differences. But what are the differences between girls and boys? From childhood we learn that "girls are made of sugar and spice and everything nice," while "boys are made of snakes and snails and puppy dog tails." What truth is there to this contrasting description of girls and boys? The fact is, there does not have to be any real truth to the description. All that is important is that parents, teachers, or others *believe* the contrasting descriptions. These beliefs themselves will trigger contrasting expectations of girls and boys and, in turn, will trigger contrasting (differential) behaviors toward them.

From the moment of birth, infant boys and girls are treated differently. Girls are dressed in pink; boys are dressed in blue. Girls wear little, frilly, lace-trimmed dresses, hardly conducive to active play. Boys wear jeans and other durable clothes designed to withstand active play. We hold and cuddle girls; we tease and roughhouse with boys. Girls are soothed and comforted when experiencing pain. Boys are told to handle pain by "acting like a man" (e.g., when getting a shot at the doctor's office or falling off a tricycle).

Girls are given so-called girl-appropriate toys, and boys are given so-called boy-appropriate toys. If you don't know which toys are which, simply visit your local chain toy store. The boy's toys will be in one section, and the girl's toys will be in another section. When asked why the toys are separated, toy store representatives respond by saying, "We are just arranging the toys the way the public wants." It could be argued that traditional preferences of toys by boys and girls reflect an early internalizing of gender role expectations (Boston, 1985).

In preparation for female adulthood, girls are encouraged to role-play a limited number of often caring-oriented careers such as nurse, teacher, mother, and housewife. In preparation for male adulthood, boys are encouraged to role-play more active, often more respected and higher-paying careers such as policeman, doctor, lawyer, scientist, and engineer.

To the extent that the nurturing of children contributes to what kind of adults they will grow up to be (nature versus nurture), how they are treated as children makes a great deal of difference. Adults' expectations of what girls and boys can and should do trigger the adults' differential behaviors toward the boys and girls. The effects of these differential behaviors is felt for a lifetime.

## WHAT THE SFP RESEARCH HAS TO SAY

Self-fulfilling prophecy research mirrors real-life SFP experience. It should come as no surprise that teachers' perceptions of students' behaviors form a significant element of teachers' academic judgments. When teachers view the former (good or bad behaviors), they predict (expect) the latter (good or bad academic performance). In a study of 800 kindergarten through Grade 2 public and parochial students, Bennett, Gottesman, Rock, and Cerullo (1993) found that students who exhibit good behavior are judged by teachers to be academically superior to students who exhibit bad behavior, regardless of the students' gender. But, as is often the case in classrooms, male subjects were consistently seen as behaving less adequately than female subjects. As a result, "teachers' perceptions of boys' academic skills were more negative than their perceptions of girls' capabilities" (p. 351).

"Wait-time," the amount of time teachers allow before providing the correct answer or calling on another student, and "incidence of teacher-call," how often students are called upon to answer, were two of the variables researched by Gore (1981). The results of this study, using 155 Arkansas fourth-grade students during mathematics instruction and five female public school teachers, were that both teacher wait-time and incidence of teacher-call favored male students. Hwang (1993), too, found that elementary teachers provided significantly more wait-time for male than for female students.

Providing a longer wait-time for boys in these mathematics classes conveys to them that the teacher expects that they know the answers. Calling upon boys more often also conveys to them that they had better be prepared because the odds are they will be called upon. These teacher behaviors reinforce "the belief that males can do almost anything if they put forth the effort" (Lindley and Keithley, 1991). Is it any wonder, then, that males do well in mathematics, that is, outscore females on the Scholastic Aptitude Test (SAT) (Dauber, 1987), and more often than girls choose math-oriented careers?

Gender-based bias in teacher expectations is not limited just to mathematics classes. Shepardson and Pizzini's (1992) research shows that science teachers also appear to treat boys and girls differently. After suggesting that there is some evidence that boys and girls may differ in their scientific abilities, Shepardson and Pizzini hypothesize that "teachers, consciously or subconsciously, provide differential educational treatment of boys and girls during science, resulting in the failure of girls to sufficiently develop their scientific abilities" (p. 147). The authors cite specific gender-based differential teacher behaviors, including female students' being called upon, praised, and criticized less often than male students and rarely being asked to give a scientific demonstration or to manipulate scientific equipment. What makes matters even worse is the fact that the elementary teachers who held higher scientific expectations for boys were themselves female. One can only wonder at the negative impact upon female students of observing female teachers exhibiting higher expectations for male students.

Sadker and Sadker's ongoing research supports the fact that teachers interact with male students—in ways likely to convey positive expectations—more often than they do female students. The title of their recent book, *Failing at Fairness: How Our Schools Cheat Girls* (1994), states their position well. Some of the paragraph headings of this book are "Pretty Is—Handsome Does" (it is clear who the doers are), "Silent Losses" (guess who is more silent, males or females), "Out of Sight, Out of Mind" (guess which gender is slighted in the curriculum no matter the subject area), and "Test Dive" (guess who, males or females, begins school testing ahead and leaves the others far behind). These headings point out how gender dependent a child's education is in our nation's schools.

In handwriting, a skill required of all students in all subject areas, gender differences emerge. Generally, teachers assign higher grades to work in good handwriting whether completed by males or females. In effect, no matter the subject knowledge being assessed, the quality of a student's handwriting influences the assigned grade. In a recent study (Sprouse & Webb, 1994) in which teachers evaluated students' spelling papers and essay samples, "100% of the elementary school teachers surveyed attributed illegible handwriting to a male, even if the paper was actually written by a female" (p. 18). The authors further state that "since illegible samples tended to be attributed to males, the grades of males may suffer due to the Pygmalion Effect" (p. 18).

In a study designed to measure whether teachers' ratings (i.e., expectations) of student performance were biased by student characteristics, Kehle, Bramble, and Mason (1974) found that of the four independent variables—students' sex, race, intelligence, and attractiveness—"only the sex of the child produced a main effect" (p. 58). "Significant effects were obtained for the sex by attractiveness interaction, and the sex x intelligence x race x attractiveness interaction" (p. 58). Gender, then, seems to be the common element upon which expectations are formed.

Is there a correlation, perhaps even a cause-and effect-relationship, between what teachers believe (i.e., expect) and what students achieve? In a study by Palardy (1969), 63 first-grade teachers first were divided into two groups based upon their expectations of how well male students, as compared to female students, could learn to read. Group A teachers believed that boys were less successful than girls in learning to read. Group B teachers believed that boys were as successful as girls in learning to read. After a semester of reading instruction, students' success in reading was measured (i.e., word reading, paragraph meaning, and word-study skills). When teachers believed boys to be less successful than girls in learning to read, boys were less successful. When boys were believed to be as successful as girls in learning to read, the boys performed as well as girls. Teacher expectations were realized; the self-fulfilling prophecy was demonstrated.

A pair of studies by Dvir, Eden, and Banjo (1995) focused upon males and females, respectively, trying to produce the Pygmalion effect rather than having the Pygmalion effect impact upon them. Some surprising results emerged from these studies. Randomly assigned male and female Israeli Defense Force cadets, in gender-segregated platoons, were led by either male or female officers. The Pygmalion effect was confirmed when males led males and when males led females, but not confirmed when females led females. In this study there were no males led by females.

In their introduction, Dvir, Eden, and Banjo (1995) cite studies from other fields, including nurses (King, 1971), clerical trainees (Eden & Ravid, 1981), and retail salespersons (Sutton & Woodman, 1989), where, "when women dominated the sample, the Pygmalion effect has not been produced" (p. 255). In their concluding statement, the authors suggest that the Greeks did not err in casting a woman as a Galatea (capable of being changed) and a man as a Pygmalion (capable of doing the changing). Eden (1990b), with Greek mythology and Shaw's modern play as a basis, describes males as *expecters* and females as *expectees*, with the latter surrendering to the expectations of the former. Could such expectation-role differences perpetuate, and even exacerbate, gender inequities—especially in the workplace? "Yes," say Hackett, Mirvis, and Sales (1991).

In another reference to the workplace, Heilman and Saruwatari (1979) explored the idea that career opportunities for workers differed for attractive women and men, especially when the job was at a managerial level. "As predicted, attractiveness consistently proved to be an advantage for men but was an advantage for women only when seeking a nonmanagerial position" (p. 360). In fact, "there was a distinct tendency for attractiveness to work *against*, rather than in favor of, female applicants" (p. 369).

Although this book is supposed to be looking at the effects of expectations, that is, the Pygmalion effect, on children in schools and not adults in the work world, surely how males and females are treated (and respond) as adults is heavily influenced by their pattern of treatment as children. Are teachers and parents treating male and female children in ways that encourage males to grow up to be Pygmalions and females to become Galateas? Clearly, more research needs to be conducted on what appear to be gender differences in generating the Pygmalion effect.

If school is, in part, a preparation for the adult world of work, what effect does a student's gender have on a teacher's prediction of occupation for that student? Moore and Johnson (1983) asked a group of teachers to assess what

level of occupation they expected 500 third-grade and 500 sixth-grade students
to achieve as adults. The choices were unskilled laborer, skilled laborer, clerical,
managerial, and professional. The authors conclude that a "significant sex bias
is present in teachers' occupational expectations for their students" (p. 473).
Males were expected to enter unskilled, skilled, and managerial occupations,
while females were expected to hold lower paying and lower status, gender-
traditional clerical positions.

Because teachers hold these expectations, one would expect that they would
convey them to students via differential treatment of male and female students.
The impact of these gender-based teacher expectations apparently is being felt
by students. When 1,000 high school students were asked to form expectations
about their future occupational salaries, female students regularly provided lower
salary estimates than males. Female students appeared "more inclined to deflate
their occupational worth" (Morrison, Bell, Morrison, Murray, & O'Connor,
1994). In our nation's schools "the evidence of clear advantage for boys and
disadvantage for girls is compelling and alarming" (Schmuck & Schmuck, 1994,
p. 23). Unequal teacher expectations continue to exist for male and female
students.

If individuals tend to get the salaries that they expect to receive (Major,
Vanderslice, & McFarlin, 1984), then, according to Morrison and colleagues
(1994), female students who deflate their future occupational worth are likely to
get just what they expect—a salary lower than their higher-expectation male
counterparts. Without some control of teacher expectations in the classroom,
females will continue to be disadvantaged. The so-called level playing field does
not exist.

## A TIME FOR INTROSPECTION—WHAT ARE YOUR EXPECTATIONS?

As a preservice or in-service teacher, what expectations do you or any of
your colleagues form, if any, regarding students based upon their gender? If you
or your colleagues don't form any, you are probably the exception. To what
extent do you act on these expectations, that is, treat male and female students
differently?

Do you assign tasks on some gender basis? Does it just seem natural to
assign the heavier and dirtier tasks (i.e., carry this, move that) to the "stronger
sex" and the more domestic activities (i.e., wash this, clean that, serve this) to
the "weaker sex"? When leaders are selected, whether for a classroom or a
playground activity, are males more often chosen than females? When creative
activities (i.e., decorating for an upcoming holiday) are undertaken, are females
more likely than males to be called upon?

When you conduct demonstrations, are males more often asked to assist you
and females more often asked to be "recording secretaries"? Do you let female
students get away with inappropriate behavior that you would discipline male
students for? If you are female, do you catch yourself identifying more with the

female students than with the male students?  And the list of questions goes on and on.

# CHAPTER 5

# RACE (AFRICAN-AMERICAN) AND THE SFP

## INTRODUCTION

"Justice is blind." False! Justice it is not blind. Persons of color tend to receive more as well as more intense punishment by the nation's courts when they break society's rules than do their fellow white citizens. "Well, at least the job market is color-blind; people are hired, as well as promoted, on merit alone." False! The job market is not color-blind. Persons of color tend to get hired as well as promoted less often than do their Caucasian counterparts. "Certainly food and housing are available equally, to all American citizens who can afford them, regardless of the color of their skin." False! Restaurants that quickly serve white patrons make persons of color wait, and apartments advertised as being available suddenly become unavailable when persons of color make inquiries. "At least in schools, teachers treat all students the same regardless of the students' race." False! Among other practices, students of color are placed in lower academic tracks when undeserved as well as disciplined more and more harshly than their white student peers (Murray & Clark, 1990).

Not all that long ago, I had a telephone call from a man who owned the home next to me. The gist of the conversation was that he was thinking of renting the home to a black family, and he wanted to know if that was okay with me—a white male. Perhaps the saddest part of this story was that the less-than-enlightened man who phoned was a respected educator in the community. Surely, this same disgusting scenario has been played out in other communities where the prospective home buyer or renter was Asian, Jewish, Italian, handicapped, and so forth.

Race is one of those distinguishing human characteristics that, unlike one's religion, ethnicity, or socioeconomic status, can't be easily hidden from view. Thus, barring any other knowledge that you might possess about someone you see for the first time, you immediately know his or her race. Knowing another person's race, though, is not the problem. The problems are the expectations (bias, prejudice, predisposition) one forms based upon that person's race and the subsequent differential behaviors toward that person. Minority students are often the focus of negative teacher expectations and corresponding negative expectation effects (McCormick & Noriega, 1986).

## WHAT THE SFP RESEARCH HAS TO SAY

Success in school and later on in life often depends upon how successful one is in learning to read. No surprises here. What may surprise readers, though, are the results of a study by Bonner-Douglas (1987). In this study, participants initially were surveyed as to their beliefs regarding how important reading was. All participants, including parents of unsuccessful readers, viewed reading as important. When parents of poor, black students were surveyed regarding how likely it would be that their child would earn high or low grades, "of the 30 parents of successful readers, 29 felt that their children were capable of earning A or B grades. Of the 30 parents of unsuccessful readers, 17 felt their children capable of getting Cs or less" (p. 8). Parents of successful readers expected more of their children; parents of unsuccessful readers expected less. It would be amazing if these expectations were not conveyed to the children.

Teachers, too, formed expectations of later success based on how well these black students could read. When asked how likely it would be that a child would complete high school and college, significantly more teachers predicted (i.e., expected) that successful readers, as compared to unsuccessful readers, would do so. It could be that the teachers were simply acknowledging the obvious—reading skills correlate with academic success. If you do not master the first, it is unlikely that you will achieve the second. But what if the teachers' predictions prompted their differential treatment of children? Then, at least according to the self-fulfilling prophecy, the teachers themselves would play a major role in helping their own predictions to be realized.

What teachers expect of students influences what students come to expect of themselves (Rice, 1990)—no matter what the color of the students' skin and, it appears, no matter what the level of education. In a study of 172 marginal black freshmen college students (marginal meaning those with low Scholastic Aptitude Test scores and weak high school GPAs), Haynes (1981) concluded that the expectations teachers have of such marginal students influences their academic achievement. Further, it was concluded that students' self-expectations (i.e., the Galatea effect) exerted a stronger influence than did teachers' expectations. Teachers are in a prime spot to help students develop their own positive self-expectations.

Richardson and Skinner (1992) report (see Ogbu, 1978) that African Americans (as well as Mexican Americans) are graded unfairly in public schools. No matter what the actual achievement of these minority students, top grades of C were all that were awarded by teachers. A grade ceiling existed. In one scenario, the researchers describe the experience of a black female graduate-student's grade plight. The student claimed, "I had one instructor who gave me a C because she thought that most blacks needed C's and that we're used to getting C's" (Richardson & Skinner, 1992, p. 36).

What perceptions, if any, do black students have of their teachers' treatment of them? To answer this question, Marcus, Gross, and Seefeldt (1991), using the Teacher Treatment Inventory (Weinstein, 1984), inventoried a group of 40 black and 40 white fifth-grade students from an affluent suburban mid-Atlantic public school system. The good news in this study was that there was no significant difference found in how black and white students perceived their teachers' treatment of them. The bad news is that when the data were analyzed by gender, black males perceived that their teachers treated them in ways that were usually reserved for lower achieving students. Black males reported that their teachers "expected less from them, called on them less scolded them for not trying and for not listening gave them more negative feedback" (p. 366) than the teachers did for whites and for black females.

One aspect of education where blacks (as well as other minorities) may be especially at risk because of teachers' expectations is in the dispensing of punishment. Do teachers punish according to race? A recent article by Hull (1994) in *Time* magazine describes a large, midwestern school system's junior high "dungeon," or in-school suspension room, located adjacent to the basement boiler room. Sentenced students remain in this hot, windowless room throughout the entire day as punishment for school infractions. Germane to this book is the fact that "black students are twice as likely to end up in the dungeon as white students; in fact, black students are twice as likely to end up disciplined throughout the entire public school system" (p. 30).

Is it possible to substitute one's achieved status for one's perceived birth-ascribed status? In other words, do teachers evaluate students more by what they actually achieve than by what, according to their skin color, they may be expected to achieve? One would hope that the answer is yes. Smith (1989), though, cites evidence to the contrary. In Smith's study, findings indicate the presence of a modified caste system where students' academic success is predicted by teachers from the students' skin color. Teachers attributed black students' underachievement to cultural deprivation and lack of parental interest. These two purported causes for underachievement, as well as others highlighted by White-Hood (1994)—no interest in school and no future goals—lacked any real, firsthand teacher knowledge. Teachers need to learn more about racial and ethnic families before they form unwarranted assumptions.

When it comes to teachers' expectations of students, not all teachers hold the same expectations. Beady and Hansell (1981) studied whether the race of teachers in black elementary schools was associated with teachers' expectations of student achievement. The answer was yes. For instance, "Black teachers had significantly greater expectations that their students would successfully enter and complete college than white teachers" (p. 196).

When a school's culture (i.e., teachers' culture) comes up against an urban black culture, "teachers need to set the same high academic standards and expectations for black students that they should set for all students, and then they need to hold students strictly accountable for meeting those standards," (Gilbert & Gay, 1985, pp. 133–134). Otherwise, "a self-fulfilling prophecy is set in motion, as teachers expect black students to fail regardless of their actual academic potential and so adjust their own behavior in ways that help realize these expectations" (p. 136).

## A TIME FOR INTROSPECTION—WHAT ARE YOUR EXPECTATIONS?

As a preservice or inservice teacher, what expectations do you or your colleagues form, if any, regarding students based upon their race? If you or your colleagues don't form any, you are probably the exception. To what extent do you act on these expectations, that is., treat students differently based upon their race?

Does race enter into your thinking when forming work group by being sure to form groups of just one race or by being sure to form groups where minorities are evenly distributed? Either strategy for forming groups is one based upon students' race. Do you direct issue-type questions (e.g., "What would minorities think of such and such governmental decision?") to members of a specific race as if those minorities (e.g., African-Americans) are in a position to speak for all members of their race? If you do, you are letting race enter into your questioning strategies.

Does you disciplining of students vary by race, for instance, minorities receiving more harsh discipline more often or receiving less harsh discipline less often than their nonminority peers? Either way, if all other factors are equal, race may have entered into your discipline formula. Being aware that race may be a factor in disseminating discipline, privileges, assignments, and so forth, is the first step in bringing the self-fulfilling prophecy under control.

# CHAPTER 6

# ETHNICITY AND THE SFP

## INTRODUCTION

"All Latinos are good lovers." "Most Brits are a bit stuffy." "All French citizens despise American tourists." "Scots are more than a bit frugal with their money." "Each and every Japanese student tests well in mathematics and science." "White men can't jump!" (Last quote is from a recent basketball movie with Woody Harrelson). Are these true statements? Sure, at least for *some* Latinos, Brits, French, Scots, Japanese, and white basketball players. But, these statements are also false for *some* Latinos, Brits, French, Scots, Japanese, and white basketball players.

Although America touts itself as a melting pot where people of different ethnic origins can blend together, the melting and the blending has not always been easy. For example, at the end of the nineteenth century and the beginning of the twentieth century, America needed immigrants—lots of them. Cheap labor was needed for building railroads, working in the mills, and digging coal out of the mines. Italians, Poles, Chinese, and other ethnic groups were welcomed to our shores with open arms—as laborers, but not necessarily as neighbors.

Like little enclaves, Polish, Italian, Jewish, and Czech communities as well as Chinatowns sprung up in American cities. When immigrants came to our shores they brought with them not only their strong backs, but also their ethnic-related food, dress, language, and religion. Pity the young Anglo-Saxon girl from the "right side of the tracks" who was caught trying to date the young Italian boy from the "wrong side of the tracks." Pity the hard-working young Polish man who tried to break into a union dominated by non-Poles.

In schools, immigrant children faced numerous problems, not the least of which was having teachers who looked down their noses (i.e., conveyed negative expectations) at these strange-sounding, strange-looking, and sometimes, strange-smelling youngsters. The lack of parent-teacher interaction, certainly hindered by parents who could not speak English, did not help matters.

## WHAT THE SFP RESEARCH HAS TO SAY

Culturally, how are ethnic minority children any different from the mainstream (Anglo), middle-class teachers and administrators who run today's schools? Would knowing the distinctive traits of minority students better prepare educators to enter classrooms? Vasquez (1990) says yes. He argues, for instance, that Hispanic children possess several traits that potentially could bring them into conflict with mainstream peers and teachers.

As one example, Vasquez (1990) points out that Hispanic children, especially Chicanos, prefer "activities in which they can achieve a goal with other students, not in competition with them" (p. 299). This attitude toward competition flies in the face of mainstream teachers and students, who believe in the survival of the fittest, and have no qualms about achieving at another's expense.

As another example, Vasquez (1990) points out that ethnic role models (e.g., especially within the professions) for Hispanics are almost nonexistent. It may be harder for Hispanic students (and their teachers) to set high academic and career goals since they believe, realistically, they will never be able to achieve them. The author goes on to present other selected trait differences and preferred learning styles for mainstream teachers and their black and Native American students.

The idea that a cultural difference can exist between mainstream teachers and minority students and parents also was revealed in a study by Paine (1981). Using a sample of 126 preschool teachers and 202 mothers, Paine assessed the subjects' expectations for white, black, and other ethnic preschoolers. "Significant differences existed between Caucasian, Black, and other ethnic subjects, with Caucasians preferring self-direction more" (p. 2927). It is not surprising that teachers, like the Caucasian subjects, preferred students to exhibit self-direction rather than conformity. The effects of ethnicity upon expectations may extend beyond the classroom to the sports arena (Solomon et al., 1996).

It is almost as if teachers believe a positive halo effect exists for some students (i.e., Asians) and a negative halo effect exists for other students (i.e., blacks, Hispanics). Some students are seen as destined for greatness, others are not. The relationship between students' ethnicity and teachers' occupational expectations for these students was the focus of a study by Moore and Johnson (1983). In their study, 500 Anglo, Hispanic, black, and Asian elementary students' future occupational status was predicted by teachers. Among the findings was the fact that "Asian students were likely to be classified into higher occupational categories on the prestige continuum than other ethnic groups" (p. 472). On the contrary, "Black students were more likely to be assigned to the unskilled labor category" (p. 472).

Bonetati's research (1994) concludes that teachers do not expect Mexican-American children or other minority children as a group to excel in school.

Ethnic bias exists and, through the self-fulfilling prophecy, is likely to be conveyed to students. Teachers also do not expect Hispanic parents, perhaps due to language barriers or unfamiliarity with the school system, to get involved in their children's education (Gault, 1989).

When expectations are low, as they are in schools for many ethnic minorities, one can expect students to "live down" to those expectations. School becomes a hostile place where only failure—and more failure—is expected, first by the teachers and then by the students themselves. Soon school is seen as a place from which to escape, from which to drop out. Among the factors principals believe contribute to high Hispanic student dropout levels are low achievement, lack of parental support, truancy, and low teacher expectations (Meza, 1986). Might it be that low teacher expectations "cause" the other factors?

One's ethnicity often is revealed in one's language. In schools, bilingual education is usually provided to nonmainstream Americans. Does students' bilingual designation influence teachers' expectations of the children's academic performance? Delgado-Contreras's (1985) research investigated just this question. In this researcher's study, teachers of first- and second-grade students had lower expectations of students with lower English proficiency. Apparently these teacher expectations had some impact, because those students predicted to have high achievement actually scored higher on standardized reading tests.

Apparently, even among Spanish-speaking students themselves, teachers' expectations vary by whether the students employ standard Spanish or nonstandard Spanish. Both bilingual teachers and bilingual teaching candidates rated standard Spanish-speaking pupils more favorably (Bloom, 1991).

Canadian teachers, too, appear to have different expectations for different ethnic groups of children. Clifton, Perry, Parsonson, and Hryniuk (1986) studied six ethnic groups (308 students) of junior high students from three schools in the diverse city of Winnipeg, Manitoba. Twenty-one teachers responded to a questionnaire designed to measure students' normative and cognitive behavior. "The results indicate that teachers' expectations of their students are affected by the students' ethnicity" (p. 65). Even more telling is their finding that "students' academic performance is consistently and highly related to the teachers' expectations" (p. 62). Teacher expectations, then, do influence student performance.

Even before teachers have formally met their minority students, they may have formed negative expectations of them. How is this possible? Students' records, complete with enough information to identify students' ethnicity, among other things, normally would be available to teachers before the start of the school year.

In a study by Demetrulias (1991) with 500 teachers in training enrolled in a private midwestern university and a public university in the West, subjects were asked to evaluate the desirability of a proposed new multicultural textbook. As part of the experimental design, different authors' names were used for the text, including both mainstream Christian surnames such as Armstrong and

Miller, and ethnic surnames such as Chin and Rodriquez. Mean ratings of the surnames revealed that both midwestern and western future teachers rated the text by Rodriquez the lowest. The text authored by Chin was rated the highest by western subjects and next to the bottom by midwestern subjects. The author names Miller and Armstrong were rated the highest by midwestern and next highest to the name Chin by western reviewers. Ethnicity, at least as suggested by an author's name, does influence others' expectations.

What can we expect from ethnic minority students? In a story told by Hall (1993) of a student teacher's experience in a high school social studies class with a Native American, the answer must be, "not much." When inquiring as to why a student, Robert, didn't participate in class discussions, the student teacher's class supervisor said, "You'll never hear him speak. He's an Indian, and Indians are too lazy to ever try and keep up with the class" (p. 180). Luckily, this story had a happy ending.

The student teacher refused to accept the supervisor's "words of wisdom" and instead treated Robert like he treated all the other students—with high expectations. By the end of the student teaching experience, Robert had lived up to those expectations. Unfortunately, there are too many Roberts out there living down to others' expectations. The negative impact (e.g., Department of Education, 1990; Johnson, 1991) of the self-fulfilling prophecy upon Native Americans, as well as other minorities, is clear.

Then again, being a minority student might be an advantage. For instance, Yamagata-Noji (1987) analyzed the questionnaire results of 180 Japanese-American college students. They found that "teachers were reported to hold only positive expectations of Japanese-American students: that they are well-behaved, smart, quiet, and that they get good grades" (p. 2561). If teachers have a stake in having their preconceived notions (i.e., expectations) come true, then, at least for Japanese-American students, the future looks bright. For most minority students, the future may not be so encouraging.

While teachers may typically perceive Asian students as successful, and this can be a real plus when it comes to influencing teachers' expectations, Bannai (1980) points out a potential problem. The author argues that "the self-fulfilling prophecy of the stereotypical, successful Asian-American student does mask real and fundamental problems in spoken communication skills" (p. 1455). Real spoken communication problems could go undiagnosed and, therefore, untreated.

"Given the linguistic and ethnic diversity of our nation's schools, teacher educators must assist teachers in unmasking stereotypical attitudes in whatever form they are clothed, superficial or otherwise, and in understanding the ways in which stereotypical perceptions are detrimental to the education of their students" (Demetrulias, 1991, p. 42). The predictions are that we will, for the foreseeable future, continue to have white middle-class educators teaching ever more diverse student bodies. Student distinctiveness, whether racial or ethnic, then, is a matter that must be addressed by educators.

## A TIME FOR INTROSPECTION—WHAT ARE YOUR EXPECTATIONS?

As a preservice or in-service teacher, what expectations do you or your colleagues form, if any, regarding students based upon their ethnicity? If you or your colleagues don't form any, you are probably the exception. To what extent do you act on these expectations, that is., treat students differently based upon their ethnicity?

Do you have any tendency to size-up a new crop of students in your classroom by their ethnicity? As you first scan the student roster and see names such as Kowalczyk, Sknoieczka, Wojnakowski, or Woinelowicz, do you immediately think "Polish" and remember all the jokes at their expense that you have heard throughout the years? When you see other student names such as Goldberg, Jacobs, Klein, Stein, and Steinberg, does an entirely different picture form in your mind—just for a second—of Jews and the value they place on of scholarship? Could you almost guess which part of the community the Skonieczkas and the Steinbergs come from?

Are you somewhat surprised when one of your Chinese, Korean, or Japanese students does not do well but less surprised when one of your Jones, Brown, or Smith students (from a nearby minority housing project) does poorly? If the answer is yes to any of these questions, then you could be guilty of abusing the self-fulfilling prophecy.

# CHAPTER 7

# GIVEN NAME AND SURNAME AND THE SFP

## INTRODUCTION

The phrase "Sticks and stones will break my bones, but names will never hurt me," must have been coined by someone who never had to endure the hurtfulness and ridicule of being called a demeaning or derogatory name. Envision the hurt of the overweight child ridiculed by words such as, "Fatty, fatty, two by four; can't get through the schoolhouse door," or the Afro-American child who is taunted by being called "nigger," or the Jewish student being called "kike." Many children don't have to imagine being called such names; they are called them every day in school.

Surely such humiliating and belittling name-calling, especially if it occurs on an ongoing basis, can hurt more than a schoolyard bully's punching or kicking (Cullingford & Morrison, 1995). When such name-calling follows a person through his or her schooling, the results cannot be shrugged off easily (Figure 7.1). Unfortunately, teachers too often keep silent about name-calling. Cohn (1987) argues that teachers' silence, whether because they don't regard name-calling as important or because acknowledging it seems too dangerous (e.g., stepping in between certain racial and ethnic groups who are hurtling insults back and forth), can be regarded as acceptance.

It appears clear that "your name is your fate" (Andersen, 1977, p. 15). "A Boy Named Sue," a country hit from years ago, has Johnny Cash realizing by the end of the song that his dad purposefully had given him a girl's name because his father knew he would not be around to help the boy grow up to be big and strong. Because of what others tend to think (expect), his father knew that in his community, any boy named Sue would have to be tough in order to overcome the hostile treatment that such a name for a male would elicit. If you recall, though, Johnny Cash ends his song by declaring that he would *never* name his son Sue!

**Figure 7.1**
**"I told you that we should not have named him Rufus."**

The song "A Boy Named Sue" simply reflects real life—then and now. One's name often carries with it a stereotype; it establishes a set of expectations that others have for someone with that particular name. What pictures (set of expectations) come to mind when you think of a boy named Clyde, Elmer, Harold, Irving, Leo, Rufus, or Wallace, or a girl named Bertha, Estelle, Gertrude, Gladys, Isidore, Louise, Nellie, or Sydonie? Contrast the pictures you have of these children with the visions conjured up for boys named David, John, Richard, and Michael (the most popular name in America for over a decade), or girls named Anne, Ashley, Jennifer, Kimberly, and Rebecca.

All other things being equal, do children's given names make any difference at all in the expectations teachers hold for students' behavior, ability, and achievement? I can tell you that the answer is yes. The answer is so unequivocally yes that we named our son David and our daughter Rebecca even though there is no one in our immediate family (i.e., parent or rich uncle or aunt) who has either of those names. According to Andersen (1977), the name David conjures up visions of "an achiever," "an undeniable winner" (p. 161), and a "beloved one" (p. 201). Our daughter's name, Rebecca, summons up similar positive visions. Although our family is not Jewish, both names (David and Rebecca) have a Hebrew ancestry which, in the eyes of many beholders (i.e., teachers), invokes a vision of a family that values education. This is, in fact, just the image we wanted to create in the eyes of beholders. Of course, as most people know, even having a scholarly name does not guarantee academic success.

Any student of history knows that many Eastern and Southern European families who immigrated to the United States around the turn of the century Americanized their names. They were aware of the negative expectations that were associated with many of their original names.

Being basically white skinned, unlike blacks and Asians, permitted these immigrants to carry off the name change successfully. With their newly acquired or changed names and after a generation or two, complete with public schooling that tended to dismiss the ways of the old country, these immigrants looked (at least sounded) as if their ancestors had come across the Atlantic with the Puritans. What's in a name? Possibly everything! "Names play a role of some importance in our mental life, and may even influence our conduct in subtle ways which we often fail to recognize" (Flugel, 1930, p. 208). A recent NBC "Dateline" program (May 21, 1996) featured a segment stressing the importance of choosing just the right name for one's child.

## WHAT THE SFP RESEARCH HAS TO SAY

Johnny Cash in his song "A Boy Named Sue" knew it, and research confirms it: certain social handicaps are thrust upon the child who carries a socially undesirable name (McDavid & Harari, 1966). Because there has emerged a "general tendency toward negative evaluation of infrequently encountered names, a parent might think twice before naming his offspring for Great Aunt

Sophronia" (p. 458).

Having college students vote to select a beauty in and of itself may seem to have little application to teachers and students. But when one realizes that the selection of a beauty queen hinged upon having a "preferred" first name, the application to the classroom becomes more obvious. Garwood, Cox, Kaplan, Wasserman, and Sulzer (1980) provided 200 college students with six photographs of women previously judged to be equivalent in physical attractiveness. Half of the photographs carried desirable first names, such as Kathy, Jennifer, and Christine, and half carried undesirable names, such as Ethel, Harriet, and Gertrude. "When physical attractiveness is held constant, judgments of such attractiveness are influenced by first-names" (p. 433). It made no difference whether the judges were male or female.

In an often-used format for a study testing the effect of name stereotypes on teachers' expectations, Harari and McDavid (1973) asked experienced teachers to evaluate student assignments, in this case short essays that had been written by fifth graders. The researchers randomly assigned common (popular) and uncommon (unpopular) names as the authors of these essays. Did students' names make any difference in the teachers' evaluations? "For teachers, the effect of the author's name upon the score assigned the essay was significant for boys and girls" (p. 223). The boy's name David was the name associated with the essay scoring the highest average.

In a 1974 study (Garwood & McDavid), 150 white, black, and Spanish teachers were asked to rate their impressions of typical student first names. Results indicated that raters across all three ethnic groups exhibited likes and dislikes for student first names. "For male names, David, Michael, Robert, and Steven, all are rated positively by all ethnic groups" (p. 4). The names Harold and Stanley, on the other hand, were viewed positively by black teachers but connoted inactivity, badness, and femininity in the judgments of Spanish and white teachers. More than two decades later, the first name Michael, a name favored by 1,400 university students (Buchanan & Bruning, 1971), continues to be most the common name for boys.

Garwood's 1976 study, where elementary teachers rated 50 male sixth graders with desirable or undesirable first names on self-concept and school achievement measures, found that the desirable name group differed from the other group on, among other characteristics, "expectations and aspirations about achievement behavior and standardized achievement scores" (p. 482). Although most teachers may believe that their expectations are not influenced by a child's name, "there is now sufficient evidence indicating that name stereotyping is one aspect of expectancy behavior" (p. 487).

In two studies (Lawson, 1971) where 180 men and women judged a set of men's given names on the dyads good-bad, strong-weak, and active-passive, subjects rated high-frequency names such as Michael, Robert, Richard, James, and John as good, strong, and active. Other names, such as Bernard and Stanley, were rated as closer to bad, weak, and passive. If teachers today respond the same way that Lawson's subjects did, then parents should think twice about selecting an unusual name for their child.

Two decades later, Lawson (1991) had 250 male and 250 female college students measure stereotypes associated with 500 common women's names along the six dimensions of good-bad, strong-weak, active-passive, sincere-insincere, intelligent-dumb, and calm-emotional. As was the case with Lawson's 1971 study, clear stereotypes emerged. Further, significant differences in the perceptions of male and female students existed.

Ellis and Beechley (1951), in an article titled "Emotional Disturbance in Children with Peculiar Given Names," clearly convey the point of their article. Although certainly many variables can contribute to a child's becoming emotionally disturbed, the authors' "study of 1,682 case histories of child guidance patients revealed that there was a significant tendency for boys with peculiar first names to be more severely emotionally disturbed than boys with non-peculiar first names" (p. 339). Boys' peculiar first names included, among others, Arend, Barrett, Carmello, and Rockwell. No emotionally disturbed/first name pattern existed for female patients. Similar results were found for an adult population of male psychiatric patients. Murphy (1957) goes so far as to argue that "the degree of pathological disturbance varies from exaggerated shame over one's name, commonly encountered among adolescents, to extremes of psychotic proportions" (p. 91).

In a 1994 study, Levine and Willis asked 200 subjects (shoppers in a Kansas City supermarket or shopping mall) to rate each of 40 unusual and common names on a 5-point Likert scale for each of six factors—successful, moral, healthy, warm, cheerful, and gender appropriate (see Mehrabian & Valdez, 1990). "The ratings were higher for usual names for all six attributes for all raters" (p. 561), that is, for high-income blacks, high-income whites, low-income blacks, and low-income whites, Levine and Willis found. They also found that "unusual names were more likely to be found for female, Black, lower income children" (p. 566).

Just when you think you might have a handle on the connection between a person's given name and how that person might be expected to behave or perform, contradictory evidence emerges. Ford, Miura, and Masters (1984) found that "children's social competence and school achievement were unrelated to the desirability of their first names" (p. 1149). These unexpected results occurred regardless of the child's sex or age.

Steele and Smithwick's (1989) study found that when 40 college student subjects were asked to rate the desirability of eight male first names by classifying them as good-bad, strong-weak, active-passive, sincere-insincere, and intelligent-dumb, clear preferences emerged. The "good" names were, in order of preference, David, Jon, Joshua, and Gregory. The "bad" names, also in order of preference, were Oswald, Myron, Reginald, and Edmund. When 40 other college students rated these same first names, this time with a conventional suit-and-tie photograph attached, "the differences between good and bad names disappeared" (p. 521). But because most students, whether in basic (K-12) or higher education, do not run around wearing suits, first names can be assumed to influence people's (i.e., teachers') expectations.

Demetrulias's (1991) research (reported earlier, in the chapter on ethnicity and the SFP), this time with surnames rather than given names, shows that name preferences still exist. On the pretense of helping in the selection of a new text, teachers-in-training from the West and Midwest were asked to evaluate an excerpt from a book on multicultural education. Subjects were given identical excerpts supposedly written by one of seven authors—Abdullah, Armstrong, Chin, Miller, Rodriquez, Silverstein, and Walzewski. Each name was accompanied by the title "Dr."

On a scale of 1 (low) to 10 (high), midwestern respondents rated the excerpts by Miller and Armstrong the highest and those by Chin and Rodriquez the lowest. Respondents from the West rated Chin the highest, with Miller and Armstrong a close second and third, and they rated Rodriquez the lowest. At first glance it appears that there exists a geographic influence, that is, more Asians live in the West and western subjects rated the name Chin highest. This same western geographic advantage, though, does not exist for the ethnic name Rodriquez; it ranked at the bottom of both rankings. Is there any reason not to believe that if adult textbook authors are judged by their surnames, students, too, are judged according to their surnames by teachers?

It appears that, individually, given names and surnames are capable of creating expectations in the minds of beholders. What expectations are created when we pair "most appropriate" and "least appropriate" given names and surnames? Gladding (1982) found that college students evaluated male therapists (i.e., counselors) most favorably who had a "most appropriate" given name and a "most appropriate" surname. Thus, at least for therapists, their job of presenting themselves to potential clients can be affected by their given name and surname.

Those of you familiar with publication style manuals, for instance, the *Publication Manual of the American Psychological Association* (1994), are aware that author citations are to include only initials for first and/or middle names. In an attempt at racial, gender, and ethnic neutrality, these conventions for reviewing and/or citing authors' works help to ensure that readers are blind to anything but what should count—the quality and substance of the manuscript.

This caution of not using first and/or middle names is well warranted if one accepts the results of Paludi and Strayer's (1985) research. The researchers had 300 introductory psychology college students rate, on a scale of 1 (highly favored) to 5 (highly unfavored), a 1,500-word article with respect to the value of the article, its intellectual depth, the competence of the author, and the quality of the article. The articles, one each from the fields of political science, psychology of women, and education, carried one of several author names: John T. McKay, Joan T. McKay, J. T. McKay, Chris T. McKay, or no name (unauthored). Pauldi and Strayer found that when reviewers assumed that the article was written by a male (i.e., John T.), they rated it higher than if they thought it had been written by a female (i.e., Joan T.). This "pro-male" bias held even when the articles were supposedly from a feminine-dominated field (i.e., psychology of women).

## A TIME FOR INTROSPECTION—WHAT ARE YOUR EXPECTATIONS?

As a preservice or in-service teacher, what expectations do you or your colleagues form, if any, regarding students based upon their names? If you or your colleagues don't form expectations, you are probably the exception. To what extent do you act on these expectations, that is, treat students differently based upon their names?

Are you able to see immediate leadership qualities in a girl named Candy or a boy named Floyd? Can you easily picture a football quarterback named Cecil or Elmer, or does a Joe, John, Jack, Kirk, or Scott fit the quarterback picture better? Does a girl named Barbie best fit your image of the captain of the debate team or do you instead immediately wonder who the Ken in Barbie's life is? Keep in mind that one of the first things that teachers learn about students, even before they personally meet them, is their names. If first impressions are lasting impressions, then how we as teachers respond to students' names can be critical.

# CHAPTER 8

# DIALECT AND/OR PRIMARY LANGUAGE AND THE SFP

## INTRODUCTION

Not too long ago, I spent a year on sabbatical at Durham University in England. Northern England, in contrast to more popular tourist areas near London, is a very friendly place. My family and I were immediately accepted into the community, regularly invited into neighbors' homes, and frequently entertained by friends in local pubs.

John, a policeman, and Bob, a fireman, lived next door with their wives, Eileen and Lynn, respectively. John and Bob both spoke with a strong "Jordie" accent, characteristic of lifelong natives of this area. In a normal conversation, when, on my behalf, they slowed down their speech, I could understand them pretty well. But, when we went out to a pub and had had a pint or two, they spoke at their normal speed, and I could not understand a single word they said. Although their language definitely pegged them as being Jordies, it mattered little because neither man had any desire to travel outside of northern England.

If one really wants to "make it" in England, meaning securing one of the better (higher paying) jobs in government, in the professions, or in the worlds of finance and business, which are centered around the hub of London, one cannot have a Jordie accent. The good London-based jobs are taken by people who can speak English as they do on the BBC (British Broadcasting Corporation). Anyone who does not speak the BBC way is instantly pegged as second class—something very important in a class-oriented society.

During my sabbatical year, the dialect problem affected the schools of Scotland, the border of which was only 50 miles north of our home. Ironically, the problem was reported in documentaries on the London-based BBC-1 and BBC-2 television stations, by newscasters speaking the BBC way. Although Scotland is supposed to be part of Great Britain, I am not sure that the Scots agree. They have their own currency, having yet to adopt the English-accepted pound coin instead of the pound note, and they run their own school system.

The problem surfaced as an outgrowth of the fact that so much of the industry (mining, automobile manufacturing, shipbuilding, drilling for North Sea oil) in northern England and Scotland has fallen on hard times or disappeared completely, so that there are few jobs for school leavers (high school graduates). At the time, Prime Minister Margaret Thatcher was quoted as saying that people who were out of work should get on their bicycles, leave their communities, and pedal to where the jobs were. Translated, this means relocate south to the London area.

Although Scottish school leavers could travel to London in search of the good jobs, the minute they opened their mouths in a job interview, it would be obvious that they did not speak the preferred BBC version of the King's English. They would sound like, and be judged as, we might judge hillbillies who were applying for a job in the financial district of New York.

The Scottish schools, then, had a dilemma. Do they change the school system's curriculum so that students learn to speak the BBC way? Speaking the BBC way would increase the likelihood that graduates would find jobs, but it was argued that it also would destroy much of what it means to be Scottish. The Scottish culture and the Scottish language (dialect) are intertwined. To destroy one is to erode the other.

The dialect and/or primary language issue has also emerged as our nation and our nation's schools struggle with the dilemma of how much to impose Standard English on our citizens. According to Sato (1989), "The facts are indisputable: As groups, African Americans, Hawaiian Americans, and other second dialect speakers consistently underachieve academically, and children in states with a large proportion of second dialect speakers do poorly on national standardized examinations" (p. 260). On a one-to-one basis, many of these students who speak a nonstandard English are hurt by teachers' pejorative attitudes (i.e., negative expectations) regarding the children's behavior and ability.

Closer to home—in fact, across the hall from me—a young history professor colleague of mine who has a strong west Texas drawl to his speech confesses that when he presents professional papers at national conferences the audience's initial reaction is, "Who is this country-sounding bumpkin?" He must proceed well into the spirited delivery of his well-researched and strongly defended argument before the audience looks beyond his speech and pays attention to his message.

## WHAT THE SFP RESEARCH HAS TO SAY

After conducting a review of the literature, Hess (1972) concluded "Standard English is the prestige dialect of the United States. Learning a Standard English need not be psychologically damaging or alienating, is an aid to academic achievement, is helpful to economic advancement, and facilitates communication. Teaching students a Standard English is NOT racist" (p. 41). According to Hess,

"There *is* indeed value to learning a Standard English" (p. 42), not the least of which involves the Pygmalion effect whereby teachers tend to rate students by their speech characteristics.

In a study by Cecil (1988), the expectations teachers held for black children who spoke Standard English and for those who spoke black dialect were investigated. In the study, 52 randomly assigned teachers listened for five minutes to five black dialect–speaking children and to five Standard English–speaking children as the youngsters responded to a series of questions. The second graders' responses were then evaluated by teachers. Specifically, teachers were asked what they thought were the chances of the child's successfully finishing second grade, what the IQ of the student was, and how well the child was performing in reading. "Results indicated that teachers surveyed expected significantly greater overall academic achievement, reading success, and intelligence from those children who spoke Standard English than from those who spoke Black Dialect" (p. 34). The reader is reminded that these teachers' expectations were formed after listening to students speak on an audiotape for only five minutes.

In research cited elsewhere in this book, Rist (1970), as well as others (i.e., Guskin, 1970; Pugh, 1974), identified children's language, Standard American English versus black dialect, as a major criterion by which teachers judge students. In Rist's study, an urban kindergarten teacher assigned her new students to one of three available tables. The children who spoke Standard American English more frequently (i.e., just like the teacher) were seated at Table 1 (closest to the teacher) and were evaluated by the teachers as having higher academic abilities. Students who spoke more often with a black dialect were seated at Table 3 (farthest away from the teacher) and were evaluated by the teachers as having lower academic abilities. Students seated in closer proximity to the teacher thus enjoyed all the benefits—for example, greater teacher attention and higher teacher evaluations.

Ferguson (1982), a seasoned inner-city high school English teacher, commented that speaking Black English rather than Standard English will forever brand students as outsiders, even long after they have graduated. The author argued that all students should be taught Standard English regardless of their environment or background. "To do less is to make a cripple out of the black child" (p. 40).

The fact that a teacher's bias against a student's Black English dialect can trigger lowered teacher expectations and lowered student performance is, according to Masland (1979), a given. The author further argues that, at least in learning to read, having a black dialect can be a disadvantage for the children, themselves. "If the syntax of written material differs from the oral language syntax of the reader, comprehension will be negatively affected" (p. 42).

Surely, many students must experience a dilemma, if not outright alienation, when it comes to deciding between using a black dialect (something modeled for them in their homes and communities) and the school's imposition of Standard or "correct" English.     Students quickly learn—as Jesse Jackson claimed (Christensen, 1990)—that Standard English is the "cash language" in America. Christensen concluded by saying that we must teach students Standard English "because they are the ones without power and, for the moment, they have to use the language of the powerful to be heard" (p. 40). At the same time, though, students should be encouraged to question the educational system that, through its imposition of Standard English, may devalue their lifelong knowledge and experience.

Is this preference by teachers for Standard English versus Black English (i.e., dialect) simply a white-black issue? Not according to McCullough (1981). In a study designed to analyze 63 elementary school teachers' attitudes toward students who speak Black English, the researcher found "that teachers held significantly less positive attitudes toward Black English–speaking children. Black teachers, moreover, demonstrated significantly less positive attitudes than White teachers" (p. 3984). Students who speak Standard English have a distinct advantage over students who speak Black English no matter what the race of the teachers.

DeMeis and Turner (1978) asked 68 white, female elementary school teachers, from seven different schools, to listen to audiotaped responses from 12 male (some black and some white) elementary students—six speaking Black English and six speaking Standard English. Teachers then rated the students in terms of personality, quality of response, and academic ability. The researchers found, generally, that Black English-speaking students were rated lower than Standard English-speaking students. "It was also found that the effect of a student dialect was much stronger if the student was white than if he was black" (p. 84). Students who spoke Black English, or as it is sometimes called, street English, were judged less favorably by teachers no matter whether the students were black or white.

Forming expectations of another based upon his or her language is not something reserved for adults—i.e., teachers and employers. Apparently young children, too, have considerable skill in judging others by their speech. In a study using 92 black and white 8- and 9-year-old children, Light, Richard, and Bell (1978) had subjects listen to two recorded speech samples. One speaker was a southern black woman who was educated and spoke Standard English, while the other was noneducated and spoke non-Standard English. In order to focus the children's attention on the point of the study, the children first were asked whether they had ever tried to imagine what someone was like just from hearing his or her voice on the radio. In effect, they were being asked if they had ever formed expectations about someone based upon just hearing a voice. After listening to the taped speech sample, the children were asked to rate the speakers. Children rated the Standard English–speaking woman as smart, pretty, rich, and nice. The non-Standard English–speaking woman was rated as dumb, ugly, poor, and mean. Even young children "recognize on some level that non-Standard English is stigmatized" (p. 263).

Aren't we a multicultural nation? Don't we value bilingualism? E. D. Hirsch (1987), in his often-cited and controversial book *Cultural Literacy*, argued that with respect to bilingualism, we should "understand that well-meaning linguistic pluralism, which would encourage rather than discourage competing languages within our borders, is much different from Jeffersonian pluralism, which has encouraged a diversity of traditions, values, and opinions" (p. 93). Although Hirsch is not opposed to biliteracy and strongly supports—in a perfect world—the value of Americans being multiliterate, he stated that "surely the first step in that direction must be for all of us to become literate in our own national language" (p. 93). The moment children open their mouths to speak, it is clear to some (including teachers) whether or not these children are culturally literate. Once these first impressions have been formed, the almost irreversible self-fulfilling prophecy process is triggered.

Before readers too hastily conclude that we should jump right in and drill kindergarten and primary-level speakers of Black English in Standard English (as recommended by Tompkins and McGee [1983] in their article about Launching nonstandard speakers into standard English), we may want to keep in mind the cautions expressed by Daniell. Daniell (1984), in a response to Tompkins and McGee (1983), suggested that teaching Standard English "must be for the right reasons, with the right methods" (p. 503). Participating fully in the mainstream culture may not be the right reason; oral drill that asks the child to repudiate his life experience may not be the right method. One "right reason" for teaching Standard English, at least according to Pixton (1974), is "because it *is* standard" (p. 251).

If we can find the right reason and the right method, the goal of teaching children Standard English may be worthwhile. As Pixton (1974) cited, the lack of skill in the use of Standard English has increasingly been recognized as a major factor in the degree of success of a child beginning his or her formal education. An extensive review of language attitude research by Ford (1977) relative to non-Standard English supports "the contention that negative attitudes are associated with particular varieties of non-standard language, and most importantly to the education profession, that teachers seem to display a preponderance of such negative attitudes" (p. 22) This is a problem for some children.

After briefly reviewing research on teacher attitudes and expectations, specifically those related to students' language (i.e., Brophy & Good, 1970; Good & Brophy, 1978; Rist, 1970; Rosenthal & Jacobson, 1968a), Freeman (1982) stated "negative teacher attitudes toward a student's language may therefore generate teacher behavior that can lead to, or at least sustain, negative student attitudes and poor student achievement. This prophecy continues to perpetuate itself as negative teacher attitudes are reinforced by poor student oral and written language" (p. 44). The fact is that Standard English–speaking children generally are rated higher than non-Standard English–speaking children (i.e., those with black dialects or Hispanic dialects) by teachers (see Granger, Mathews, Quay, &

Verner, 1977; Politzer & Hoover, 1976; Ramirez, Arce-Torres, & Politzer, 1976; Williams, Hopper, & Natalicio, 1977).

### A TIME FOR INTROSPECTION—WHAT ARE YOUR EXPECTATIONS?

As a preservice or in-service teacher, what expectations do you or your colleagues form, if any, regarding students based upon their dialect and/or language? If you or your colleagues don't form any, you are probably the exception. To what extent do you act on these expectations, that is, treat students differently based upon their dialect and/or language?

If you were born and raised in New England, what are your first thoughts when you hear one of your newly arrived male students talk with a Senator Phil Gramm–type, west Texas drawl, or hear a blond, blue-eyed, Southern belle use her first "you all" in a sentence? Do nonsoutherners think that most southerners are a bit slow on the take because they may talk a little slower?

Do you catch yourself responding to immigrant students who have not yet mastered the English language by talking louder to them, almost as if they are hard of hearing? This, of course, is what many tourists do when they travel to other countries where the citizens might not be fluent in English. How does speaking louder help?

Do you ever associate—even for a moment—the lack of English language fluency with the lack of cognitive ability? Do you ever associate urban students' use of street language with their more likely being potential discipline problems? If you do any of these things, you probably hold different expectations for different students just because of their dialect and/or language. If you hold different expectations, you will act toward them in a differential manner, and the self-fulfilling prophecy will be off and running!

# CHAPTER 9

# ATTRACTIVENESS
# AND THE SFP

## INTRODUCTION

Beauty is good; lack of beauty is bad, sometimes downright evil. From infancy, we are schooled to believe that good and bad, smart and dumb, and clean and dirty are features, respectively associated with good-looking people and with not-so-good-looking people. In fairy tales such as "Cinderella," read to us by loving parents, we have the handsome prince and the beautiful maiden representing all that is good in our world and the ugly stepmother and stepsisters representing all that is bad. In "Sleeping Beauty," we have a beautiful princess given a poison apple by an ugly, wart-faced witch who represents evil. Beauty suggests goodness; ugliness, of course, suggests wickedness (Adams & Crossman, 1978).

In the Saturday morning cowboy serials of days past, the hero and heroine, who always won in the end, were good-looking. The bad guys were downright ugly and, with the hurrah of the audience, always lost—got caught or shot—in the end. Even if the sound failed on the television set, one did not have to be an Einstein in order to determine instantly who represented "good" and who represented "evil"! The actors simply looked the part! Good guys looked like good guys, and bad guys looked like bad guys. The message that "beauty is good," and, therefore, by inference, "ugliness is bad—even repulsive," continues to bombard us, both on television and in the cinema.

So, is there really a big problem? Surely everyone knows that fairy tales are just that—make-believe tales made up to entertain (sometimes scare) children. But do fairy tales, Saturday morning serials and cartoons, prime-time television programs, and movies do more than simply entertain? Do children learn from these media while they are being entertained? Do children learn the "beauty is good" message? If so, how does it affect children's expectations of themselves, of their peers, of their teachers, and generally, of any and all folks who can be classified as being beautiful or being ugly?

When these children grow to adulthood, do they still believe the "beauty is good" message? What evidence is there in real life that adults, in general, act on their "beauty is good" beliefs? And, more germane to the subject of this book, what evidence is there that teachers allow this "beauty is good" theory to influence their interactions with students?

Most folks recognize that beauty is in the "eye of the beholder." To the extent that beauty is something that is in the "eye of the beholder," the beholder holds expectation-type power over the beholdee! The conditions are ripe for the self-fulfilling prophecy to operate and, as a result, Pygmalions (beholders) create Galateas (those who *live up* to the Pygmalion's expectations) and Golems (those who live down to the Pygmalion's expectations).

Beauty, then, as an abstract notion, is not easy to define. Although it is not *easy* to define, it may not be impossible to do so—or at least say Langlois and Roggman (1990). They argue that there is more than a passing cross-cultural agreement as to those facial features generally judged to be attractive. The authors' data suggest that "attractive faces are those that represent the central tendency or the averaged members of the category of faces" (p. 120) used in their study. Attractive faces, then, are average faces.

The nineteenth-century researcher Sir Francis Galton also tackled the problem of defining "beautiful" and "handsome." He used a technique called composite portraiture, by which a finished picture presented to test subjects is a face that averages the features of the group. "His experiment showed that a good-looking face is one with regular, typical features; an ugly face is one with surprises" (Wilson & Nias, 1976, p. 97).

There is more than sufficient evidence to suggest that adults, in general, act toward others based upon the "beauty is good" message (Figure 9.1). The net effect of this is that attractive people are more likely to be perceived more favorably. This translates into a greater willingness on the part of others to help them, more likelihood that they will be hired, a greater probability that they will be promoted, and a greater chance that they will be treated more favorably by our court systems—all because they are attractive! After all, who wouldn't want to help "good" people?

For instance, on a recent "60 Minutes" (1994) television show, two women took turns playing the role of a stranded motorist in downtown Atlanta (see Athanasiou and Green, 1973). One young woman, through the help of makeup, was made to look less attractive. With her car hood up, obviously in need of assistance, she stood and waited as cars just whizzed by. Occasionally someone would stop and, at most, volunteer information about where she could walk to get gasoline. The other woman, although dressed the same and also obviously in need of assistance, was blond and, by society's standards, much more attractive. Cars came screeching to a stop, and men stumbled over each other volunteering to render assistance. In no time at all, the attractive woman had her gas tank half filled! No doubt, being attractive has its benefits.

**Figure 9.1**
**A Person's Looks Can Be Deceptive**

Physical attractiveness has also been shown to influence work opportunities (Miller, 1982, p. 275). In another segment of the same "60 Minutes" program, two male actors, one quite handsome and one rather ordinary looking, were provided with identical job credentials, coached on how to act the same, and then sent out on the same job interviews. With hidden cameras capturing the results, the handsome job applicant was offered the job on the spot, while the plain-looking applicant was told, "We will give you a call." No call came. When this undercover research was repeated with two women, although they were applying for a job that did not demand direct exposure to the public where looks might be important, the result was that only the attractive woman was offered the job on the spot. She also was told that the salary for the position was higher than that disclosed to the "plain Jane" job applicant.

Of all the human characteristics upon which people form expectations, none has been so widely researched as that of "attractiveness." That is one reason why this chapter is longer than many of the others. Even if we separate the human characteristic of body build from attractiveness, as has been done in this book, it is still easy to find reams of material (journal articles, conference papers, and books) discussing the effects of attractiveness upon expectations.

Although "beauty may be only skin deep," we all know that much attention is paid to those parts of us seen by other people. This is evidenced by the sales of cosmetics and the high-profile locations within department stores of cosmetic counters. If Marshall McCluhan (1964) is correct and the "medium is the message" (as those in the media would have us believe), then attention to a person's looks seems justifiable. It would be naive to believe that our preoccupation with a person's beauty stops at the schoolhouse door (Figure 9.2).

## WHAT THE SFP RESEARCH HAS TO SAY

Dion, Berscheid, and Walster (1972) found that attractive individuals were seen as possessing more socially desirable personality traits. Among the traits associated with "attractive stimulus persons" were having greater prospects for happier social and professional lives, achieving more prestigious occupations, being more competent spouses, marrying earlier, and having better marriages. Further, attractive people also were liked more, judged to be smarter, and rated higher on sharing and friendliness (Langlois & Stephan, 1977).

Can elementary teachers predict from photographs which sixth-grade students would have more positive peer relationships, evidence greater academic ability, and be better adjusted? The answer, according to Lerner and Lerner (1977), is, "Yes, just look for the more attractive students." Predictions are one thing, but are these predictions realized? The researchers cite that "evidence was found for relations among physical attractiveness, grade point average, and actual adjustment" (p. 585).

The basic building block upon which all relationships are built is the dyad—one person getting to know another person. What would happen if the

**Figure 9.2**
**First Day of School "Good Impressions"**

only way we could get to know another person was through a phone conversation? How might we act toward the unseen person on the other end of the line? How would our actions be influenced by having been told that the other person was attractive or unattractive? Could our actions influence this other person? Snyder, Tanke, and Berscheid (1977) designed an experiment to answer these questions. In their study, males, referred to as "perceivers," interacted with females, referred to as "targets," via a brief phone call. Perceivers were told that the target was either attractive or unattractive. Independent judges noted that targets designated physically attractive targets actually "came to behave in a friendly, likable, and sociable manner in comparison with targets whose perceivers regarded as unattractive" (p. 656). Even over the telephone, perceivers became Pygmalions.

In a study reported earlier in chapter 4, Heilman and Saruwatari (1979) found that the advantages of being attractive differed depending on whether one was male or female. "Attractiveness proved to be an advantage for men but was only an advantage for women when seeking a nonmanagerial position" (p. 360). Women, then, may be faced with a dilemma: remain feminine and beautiful and, as a result, achieve lower status jobs, or appear (i.e., act, dress) more masculine and increase the chances for career advancement.

Who is more worthy of help—attractive or unattractive people? Although we might like to believe that a person's looks would not enter into a decision of whom we help, Benson, Karabenick, and Lerner (1976) demonstrated otherwise. In their experiment, they placed completed identical graduate school application forms (with stamped, addressed envelopes) in public phone booths in a large metropolitan airport's central lobby. The idea was to make it appear as if the ready-to-be-mailed materials had been accidentally left behind. A personal note to the applicant's father was attached making it clear that the applicant believed his or her father would mail the application. Therefore, there was no reason to expect that the applicant would return in order to retrieve the materials.

Each application had a picture attached to it of either an attractive or unattractive male or female applicant. Approximately 600 subjects were observed entering the phone booths. The researchers report that consistent with the "beauty is good" hypothesis, attractive applicants had their materials mailed for them (i.e., received in the psychology department) at a rate of 47% as opposed to 35% for unattractive persons. Pretty, apparently, does please!

What can we tell from a student's facial attractiveness? Everything? Nothing? Something in between these two extremes? Adams and LaVoie (1974) asked 350 classroom teachers, Grades 1 through 6, to rate (predict) students on a variety of measures such as "parent involvement in schools," "peer relations," "popularity," "attitude toward school," and "work habits." A color photograph was attached to the factitious student progress reports that served as the basis for each teacher's evaluation. The students' faces, as evaluated by independent judges, varied in attractiveness from "very attractive" to "very unattractive." Surprisingly, the researchers found that "high attractive students generally received lower ratings on attitudes and work habits than low attractive students" (p. 82).

That an overall pattern of ascribing positive attributes to attractive students is the norm is shown clearly in a study by Kenealy, Frude, and Shaw (1988). Using approximately one thousand 11- and 12-year-old children from schools in Wales, the researchers had teachers rate the students first on attractiveness (photographs displayed on 35 mm color slides), and second on a series of personal characteristics (e.g., confidence, sociability). "The teachers' ratings of attractiveness correlated with their judgments of (in decreasing magnitude) children's sociability, popularity, academic brightness, confidence, and leadership" (p. 379). Clearly, teachers believed that they could predict a good deal about children from simply viewing their photographs.

Using predictor variables such as self-ratings of physical attributes along with external judgments of their facial attractiveness, approximately 300 college students responded to several standardized tests believed to measure characteristics normally attributed to physical attractiveness. Adams (1977) concluded that physically attractive people, in comparison to their less attractive peers, possessed more positive self-concepts (self-regard) and higher resistance to peer pressure.

In another study by Adams (1978), a total of 240 black and white, female Head Start preschool teachers were interviewed to determine the effects of a child's physical attractiveness on initial teacher expectations. In the interview, these teachers were shown a randomly assigned photograph of one of the children (independently judged previously as being either extremely attractive or extremely unattractive) and asked to predict how they felt the child would do in their classroom if so assigned. A child's level of attractiveness was found to influence teachers' initial expectations regarding the child's behavior and likely school success. Implications for the well-being of children who attend early intervention programs such as Head Start were highlighted.

In a study that supports much of what has been reported thus far, Clifford (1975) received usable responses from 420 first-grade teachers who had been asked to complete an opinion sheet after reviewing student progress reports that had an attractive or unattractive student photograph attached. Clifford's data indicated that "It is evident that attractive children elicited more favorable teacher expectations than less attractive children, particularly on academic achievement-related variables" (p. 203). Basically, this study replicated an early Clifford & Walster (1973) study conducted with fifth-grade teachers and students where teachers perceived attractive children more positively—as more intelligent, more likely to pursue advanced education, and more likely to have parents who value academics.

Do teachers' expectations based upon student attractiveness eventually translate into actual academic advantages? Felson's (1980) study with 17 teachers and 400 middle-school students concludes that "physically attractive children are attributed slightly more ability and assigned slightly higher grades"

(p. 70). To make matters even more unfair, it appeared that teachers not only favored the attractive children but also discriminated against the unattractive children.

Discipline, another very important aspect of the schooling experience, appears, at least to Dion (1974), to be influenced by how attractive or unattractive a child is. Dion claims that there is "supportive evidence" (p. 777) that a student's physical attractiveness influences female teachers' disciplinary behavior toward that student. "Specifically, women behaved more leniently toward an attractive boy than toward an attractive girl. In contrast to women, men's administration of penalties to a child was not influenced by the child's sex" (p. 777). Here we have, as is the case in the real world, more than one variable operating (i.e., sex and attractiveness).

Offering contrary evidence to Dion's 1974 study, Marwit, Marwit, and Walker's (1978) "analyses of student-teacher and practicing-teacher data failed to support the hypothesis that transgressions of unattractive children are rated more severely than those of attractive children" (p. 914). Rich (1975), too, found this same, perhaps unexpected, outcome—teachers judging unattractive students' misbehaviors as less undesirable than those of attractive students. Further, unattractive girls were found to receive more lenient punishments than those assigned to unattractive boys.

How old are children when they first begin to judge physical attractiveness the same way that adults do? This developmental question was stressed in a study by Cavior and Lombardi (1973). They concluded that whether they are male or female, "children begin to use similar or common criteria in judging physical attractiveness at age 6 and increase thereafter until the age of 8, when they use the same criteria as older judges" (p. 69). It appears, then, that the kindergarten through third grades can be especially important in emphasizing the criteria one's culture uses to define attractiveness.

Dion (1973) found that children's judgments, at least regarding attractive and unattractive peers, could be made even by 3- to 6-year-olds. In Dion's study, these young children not only were able to identify photographs of attractive peers (as previously designated by adults), but also chose them over unattractive children as those they would most like to have as their friends. This connection between a child's physical attractiveness and his or her popularity among peers is supported by Dion and Berscheid (1974).

In multicultural environments (increasingly the case in today's world), can we predict who will most often be perceived as beautiful and hence enjoy the benefits that accompany the "beauty is good" hypothesis? According to Camaren (1981), the answer is "yes." Her research with 30 dominant (Anglo), 30 near dominant (Italian), and 30 minority (Aboriginal) female kindergarten children revealed that the influence of the dominant culture on attractiveness preferences was extensive. All groups chose the Anglo photographs as being attractive and being associated with prosocial attributions.

In a similar vein, a recent newspaper article describes consumers' frustrations with trying to find the Happy Holidays Barbie doll (*Morning News*, 1995). The article reports that "the problem is that only the black version can easily be found, and psychologists say even black girls seem to prefer the white version of the leggy doll in her billowy green gown" (p. 1A). Once again, the dominant culture seems to define what beauty is.

Who is most to blame for promoting the "beauty is good hypothesis"— teachers, mothers, fathers? One experiment by Adams and Crane (1980) using 74 preschool boys and girls offers evidence, albeit correlational, that "mothers and teachers may be stronger agents of the physical attractiveness stereotype than are fathers" (p. 224).

Does the "beauty is good" hypothesis hold equally for males and females? Bar-Tal and Saxe's (1976) answer to this question is no. They conclude, as daily experiences confirm, that "physical attractiveness is a more important factor in the evaluation of females than in the evaluation of males" (p. 131). For instance, unattractive females have been found to have significantly higher blood pressure than attractive women—a relationship not found among unattractive and attractive men (Hansell, Sparacino, & Ronchi, 1982). Being attractive can be an advantage for both sexes, but, "while unattractive females are judged negatively in almost all cases, unattractive males are sometimes evaluated positively" (p. 126). As Miller (1970) claims, "if one must be unattractive, it is a better fate to be male than female" (p. 242). Things have changed little since his pronouncement!

In another study examining the attractiveness of male and female students and students' academic performance, once again, attractive females seemed to lose. Sparacino and Hansell (1979), in a study of male and female high school students, found that "attractiveness was not associated with achievement for 84 boys but was negatively associated for 83 girls" (p. 449). These findings, then, seem to challenge Dion's "beauty is good" hypothesis—at least for female students. Having said this, research by Styczynski and Langlois (1977) concluded, for middle-class nursery school children in social situations (e.g., assessed by questions such as, Who do you especially like?), that attractiveness may be a disadvantage, at least for boys.

The self-fulfilling prophecy is a two-edged sword. Most of the research cited, thus far, looks at how teachers' views of attractiveness influence their expectations (judgments) of students. What about students' views of attractiveness and the influence such views have on their expectations (judgments) of teachers? This question was investigated in a study (Chaikin, Gillen, Derlega, Heinen, & Wilson, 1978) where the same teacher, made to look attractive or unattractive, delivered the same videotaped lecture to groups of 9- and 12-year-old students. Following the videotaped lecture, students were asked to respond to a 20-item impression ratings questionnaire. The study revealed that "the teacher was evaluated much more favorably when she was presented as being physically attractive, rather than unattractive" (p. 591). In this day and age, when formal measures of teacher effectiveness regularly are solicited from students (e.g., at my institution we administer in all classes the Student Rating of Teacher Effectiveness [SRTE]), which has yet to be proven valid) and are figured into merit, promotion, and/or tenure decisions, a teacher's physical attractiveness can be a real advantage.

In a study by Goebel and Cashen (1979), black-and-white photographs of teachers were presented to 150 students in Grades 2, 5, 8, 11, and 13 (the equivalent of college freshmen). The students' task was to rate these teachers on seven factors of teacher performance. The research showed that "across all developmental levels and on all factors, ratings of unattractive teachers tended to be lower" (p. 646).

When surveyed by Hunsberger and Cavanagh (1988), elementary school students consistently chose attractive teachers "as being the nicest persons, the happiest, the ones they would learn the most from" (p. 73) and unattractive teachers as the ones "who would punish their students when they misbehaved" (p. 73). The authors found a "significant tendency for children to prefer attractive teachers" (p. 73). How a teacher looks (i.e., attractive or unattractive) is one of the first things students notice. If first impressions are lasting impressions, less attractive teachers can look forward to an uphill battle to overcome these impressions, even though they may possess obvious teaching competence.

Throughout this chapter, it has been assumed that people viewed as attractive were also viewed as good—smarter, kinder, friendlier, having higher aspirations, more likely to pursue advanced education—and that the former led to the latter. Perhaps, though, beauty does not evoke goodness; instead, maybe goodness evokes beauty, or at least so suggests Gross and Crofton (1977). Their study offers data "which clearly lend support to the more palatable possibility that those who are seen as good become more beautiful" (p. 89). Wouldn't this be a better world if beauty continued to be valued and the only way to achieve beauty would be through achieving goodness?

The term "attractiveness" as it has been used in this chapter typically refers to a person's physical looks; he or she is "good-looking" or "not good-looking." In everyday life, the term "attractiveness" can also refer to vocal or auditory stereotypes, in other words, the attractiveness or unattractiveness of the voice. Educators themselves often use a more attractive (i.e., warmer and less hostile) voice tone when they interact with students for whom they hold higher expectations (Blanck & Rosenthal, 1984). Sometimes, as highlighted by Zuckerman, Hodgins, and Miyake (1993), there may be interactions between physical and vocal attractiveness. Apparently, people would be viewed as attractive "if they were high on both physical and vocal attractiveness and were viewed as unattractive if they were low on either physical or vocal attractiveness" (p. 204).

## A TIME FOR INTROSPECTION—WHAT ARE YOUR EXPECTATIONS?

As a preservice or in-service teacher, what expectations do you or your colleagues form, if any, regarding students based upon their attractiveness? If you or your colleagues don't form any, you are probably the exception. To what extent do you act on these expectations, that is, treat students differently based upon their attractiveness?

Attractiveness is an immediately obvious human characteristic and one that adults (including teachers) seem to favor. If a child looks like your idea of an attractive student—looks, act, and dresses the part—do you show favoritism? If you don't, other teachers do. Teachers award attractive children higher grades, praise them more, criticize them less, discipline them less and less harshly, and so forth. Are you guiltless?

Do you give attractive children the benefit of the doubt over less attractive children in grading and discipline? Do you find some attractive students simply irresistible—they can do no wrong, and what wrong they do can be justified? If some students simply look the part of a good student, that is, are attractive without being flashy, do they have an advantage over other students? Should they? Only you can answer this question for your classroom.

Note, I purposefully have not included my picture in this book for fear that the book's content might be judged by my attractiveness or unattractiveness. Although we all know that "one cannot judge a book by its cover," we often do form an initial judgment of a book by the author's picture on the book jacket. Don't we?

# CHAPTER 10

# BODY BUILD
# AND THE SFP

## INTRODUCTION

Like it or not, society tells us that certain body builds are preferable to others. People with one type of body build are destined to lead; people with other types of body builds are destined to follow, and that's just the way it is!

In a walk down nostalgia lane, you might recall that in the children's western "The Cisco Kid," Cisco, the hero, had the good build; his sidekick, on the other hand, was "fat, old Poncho" (Brooks & Marsh, 1981, p. 154). On the "Wild Bill Hickok" show, Wild Bill, the handsome hero, had the good build; his sidekick, Jingles (not the most manly of names), played by Andy Devine, was overweight and could be heard at the end of each program screaming in a shrill, raspy voice, "Wait for me, Wild Bill," as Wild Bill quickly and easily outdistanced his portly partner.

On "The Andy Griffith Show," a show that has held its popularity across several generations, Andy Taylor is the well-built sheriff, the person in charge. Barney Fife, the deputy sheriff who can't even be trusted with bullets in his gun, is played by skinny-as-a-rail Don Knotts, "the most inept, hyperactive deputy sheriff ever seen on television" (Brooks & Marsh, 1981, p. 39). Don Knotts's character changed little when he later played the easily fooled landlord on "Three's Company."

Today, in the popular television program "Home Improvement," Tim Allen has an average-to-good build; his sidekick Al is overweight. On "Seinfeld," Jerry Seinfeld has the average build; his less-than-talented buddy George is overweight (he is almost bald, too). Of note is the fact that I had to ask more than ten people who regularly watch "Seinfeld" what Seinfeld's buddy's name was. I, too, had forgotten his name.

Can fat people be the stars? Can skinny people be the stars? Yes, but normally only when well-built people are missing from the cast and/or when the show is a comedy. In "The Honeymooners," we had two stars—Ralph Kramden, an overweight bus driver, and Ed Norton, a skinny, high-strung city sewage worker. Neither was depicted as being very competent; both, though, were funny and amused their audience.

On all three major television networks' morning programs, the anchors, whether male or female, in general have an average build. But on NBC's "Today Show," the less than prestigious position of weather man is held by an overweight Willard Scott (an ex–Ronald McDonald clown), and when he is not there, by Al Roeker, who also is overweight.

Look at the political candidates, both successful and unsuccessful, for the United States presidency over the past several decades—not a fat one among the bunch, not a skinny one among the bunch. In a recent newspaper article commenting upon the Massachusetts race between Ted Kennedy and Mitt Romney, the author said that "the danger is not that voters will look at Kennedy and see long nights in the barroom. The worst scenario is that they will regard him as a walking illustration of fat in the budget" (Collins, 1994, p. 3-B). The message seems to be that long nights in a barroom are okay, but being overweight cannot be tolerated!

Is there a pattern here? The overweight television and film sidekick plays the role of second fiddle, of a follower, not a leader. The overweight politician faces an uphill battle when it comes to getting elected. Is life really like this? More important in regard to the message of this book, is life really like this in the classroom?

## SHELDON'S CLASSIFICATION OF BODY BUILD TYPE

No discussion of body build would be complete without mentioning the body build type theories of William Sheldon. The research on expectations and body build type that follows looks at how people are judged with respect to their general body build or physique. Although people may gain and lose weight as they grow older, their basic body build normally remains the same. Sheldon (1940, 1942, 1954) categorized body build into three general types—endomorphic, mesomorphic, and ectomorphic.

*Endomorphs* have round, soft bodies, with a central concentration of mass. Less tactful descriptions might be that these people are "heavy," "chubby," "plump," "stout," and even "fat." Jerry Seinfeld's stocky sidekick George on the "Seinfeld" television show would be classified as an endomorph. Endomorphs are viewed as social but not socially assertive, even-tempered, trusting, and relaxed. Extreme endomorphs—obese people—are considered less attractive and often are discriminated against or stigmatized.

*Mesomorphs* have square, rugged shoulders, small buttocks, and bodies with conspicuous muscles. Jerry from the "Seinfeld" television show and Andy Griffith from "The Andy Griffith Show" would be described as mesomorphs. Mesomorphs are seen as being aggressive, socially assertive, strong, independent, energetic, good-looking, competitive, and good at physical activities. Mesomorphs, in effect, have the ideal American body build (see Lerner & Korn, 1972).

*Ectomorphs* have thin, fragile-looking bodies, drooping shoulders, and elongated, bent-forward necks. Don Knotts, who played the deputy sheriff on "The Andy Griffith Show," would typify an ectomorph. Ectomorphs are judged as being pessimistic, uncompetitive, sensitive, in need of friends, underconfident, inhibited, and nervous.

Sheldon's theories, especially those that create a parallel between a person's temperament (i.e., viscerotonic, somatotonic, and cerebrotonic) and the person's physique, have not been supported (e.g., Humphreys, 1957; Walker, 1962), or at least not strongly supported (Child, 1950), by ensuing research. However, the fact is that many people form their first impressions—often their lasting impressions—of other people based on their body build type.

Personality factors are associated with these three body types (Janssen & Whiting, 1984). One's personality, once allowed to be influenced by the expectations of others, can bias how one acts toward those who held the original expectations. It isn't, then, just that others expect people with certain body builds to act a certain way, the people, themselves, eventually expect themselves to act that way.

## WHAT THE SFP RESEARCH HAS TO SAY

Using teachers' natural perceptions (expectations), Adams and Cohen (1974) researched the impact of kindergarten, fourth-grade, and seventh-grade students' physical characteristics upon student-teacher interactions. Teachers' reactions (i.e., attentiveness and permissiveness) toward students and teachers' ratings of students (i.e., on facial attractiveness and physical appearance) were measured. It was concluded that "teachers' interactions appear to be initially influenced by physical characteristics of the child" (p. 4).

When do body build stereotypes begin to form in young children? Brylinsky and Moore (1994) asked over 300 kindergarten through fourth-grade students to rate line drawings of thin, average, and chubby body types on twelve pairs of bipolar adjectives (i.e., brave/afraid, smart/stupid, strong/weak). As predicted from similar studies (e.g., Stager & Burke, 1982), the average-build child (line drawing) was perceived as favorable, while the chubby-build child (line drawing) was seen as unfavorable. The thin-build child (line drawing) "emerged as a combination of the socially desirable traits identified with the average build stereotype and the negative physical capability traits associated with the chubby build stereotype. The unfavorable perception of the chubby stereotype appears between first and second grade" (p. 170).

No matter how you look at people, from their front, side, or rear, Collins and Plahn (1988) argue that certain body shapes are preferred over others. Using a series of black-line drawings of male and female somatotypes (ectomorph,

**Figure 10.1**
**Female Body Types: Ectomorph, Mesomorph, & Endomorph**

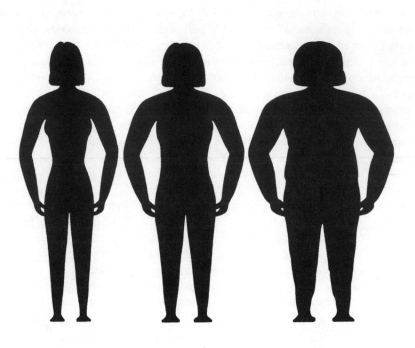

mesomorph, and endomorph), oriented three ways (front, side, and rear), a group of 160 college-level volunteers were asked, among other tasks, to select a preferred, ideal somatotype and a least preferred, aversive somatotype. Male and female subjects differed in their preference for an ideal somatotype, with females choosing the thin, ectomorphic figure and males choosing the medium, muscular, mesomorphic figure. On the contrary, male and female subjects uniformly agreed on their choice of least preferred body type—the extreme endomorphic physique.

In a study concerning the relationship between physique and reputation in adolescent boys, Hanley (1951) used approximately 120 white males as subjects. His results show an association between students' Reputation Test scores and their body build. For instance, significant correlations were found between mesomorphic physiques and such reputations as "daring," "leader," "takes chances," "bossy," "good at games," "grown up," and "real boy." In contrast, ectomorphic physiques were correlated significantly with reputations such as "unhappy," "submissive," "not quarrelsome," and "bashful." Clearly, mesomorphs enjoy a more positive set of assigned reputation traits.

Caskey and Felker (1971) report that body image stereotyping clearly is on the minds of elementary school girls. In their study using 75 girls (15 each from Grades 1–5), they had subjects respond to Staffieri's (1967) adjective list (i.e., clean, stupid, lonely) with respect to three body descriptions—ectomorph, mesomorph, and endomorph. Consistent with the outcomes of other, similar studies, the researchers found that ectomorphs (characterized by leanness) and mesomorphs (characterized by muscle), as opposed to endomorphs (characterized by excess fat), more often were assigned favorable adjectives.

The possibility that women might hold stereotypes about female body types and their relationship to personality descriptions and career choices was investigated by Keas and Beer (1992). Seventy-five female college students were provided' with drawings depicting three female somatotypes (endomorphic, mesomorphic, and ectomorphic body builds). (See Figure 10.1.) These subjects then were asked, via a series of questions that started with the words "The women who would," to respond to a list of behavioral descriptions adapted from Lerner's (1969) research with male subjects.

The results of the women's responses to the behavioral descriptions are shown in Table 10.1, "Percentage of 75 Women Choosing Endomorph (A), Mesomorph (B), and Ectomorph (C) by Item." A quick review of Table 10.1 shows that, without a doubt, the more positive behavioral descriptions are associated with mesomorphs, for example, "would be elected as a leader" (77%), "would endure pain the best" (86%), "would have many friends" (70%), and "would make the poorest doctor" (4 percent). The least positive descriptions are associated with the endomorphs, for example, "would be least preferred as a personal friend" (64%), "would make the poorest doctor" (64%), and the ectomorphs, for example, "would most likely to have a nervous breakdown" (77%), "would make a poor mother" (58%).

**Table 10.1**
**Percentage of 75 Women Choosing Endomorph (A),**
**Mesomorph (B), and Ectomorph (C) by Item**

| | Item Number and Content | A | B | C |
|---|---|---|---|---|
| **The woman who:** | | | | |
| 1. | ..is to be most wanted as a friend. | 1.3 | 76.0 | 22.7 |
| 2. | ..eats the most. | 97.3 | 2.7 | 0.0 |
| 3. | ..smokes 3 packs of cigarettes a day. | 26.7 | 2.7 | 70.8 |
| 4. | ..eats the least often. | 1.3 | 10.7 | 88.0 |
| 5. | ..needs friends the most. | 66.7 | 4.0 | 29.3 |
| 6. | ..would be most likely to have a nervous breakdown. | 20.0 | 2.7 | 77.3 |
| 7. | ..would be least preferred as a personal friend. | 64.0 | 10.7 | 25.3 |
| 8. | ..would be the most aggressive. | 16.0 | 77.3 | 6.7 |
| 9. | ..would make a poor mother. | 28.4 | 13.5 | 58.1 |
| 10. | ..has the fewest friends. | 77.3 | 4.0 | 18.7 |
| 11. | ..would drink the most. | 42.7 | 30.7 | 26.7 |
| 12. | ..would be the least aggressive. | 26.7 | 4.0 | 69.3 |
| 13. | ..would make the poorest doctor. | 64.0 | 4.0 | 32.0 |
| 14. | ..would be elected as a leader. | 4.0 | 77.3 | 18.7 |
| 15. | ..would assume leadership. | 0.0 | 92.0 | 8.0 |
| 16. | ..would not smoke at all. | 5.4 | 89.2 | 5.4 |
| 17. | ..would endure pain the best. | 9.3 | 86.7 | 4.0 |
| 18. | ..would endure pain the least. | 30.7 | 1.3 | 68.0 |
| 19. | ..would make the poorest athlete. | 78.7 | 0.0 | 21.3 |
| 20. | ..would make the best athlete. | 0.0 | 98.7 | 1.3 |

Keas and Beer's (1992) results, in general, are consistent with those found by Lerner in 1969. What this suggests is that two and a half decades later, little has changed in what we expect of people, males or females, based upon their body build. With respect to the second part of Keas and Beer's study, associating body builds with careers, some unsettling results emerged. The good occupations, the prestigious occupations, clearly correlated with one body build—mesomorph! Mesomorphic body builds were associated with such careers as stock broker, manager of a 2,000 employee factory, electrical engineer, and superintendent of schools. Ectomorphs were associated with bookkeeper, book binder, typist, and file clerk. Endomorophs were associated with garbage collector, butcher, janitor, and restaurant pastry chef.

In a similarly designed study, Spillman and Everington (1989) had a total of approximately 250 male and female undergraduates complete a questionnaire where, among other things, they assigned behavioral characteristics to one of three female body build silhouettes—endomorph, mesomorph, and ectomorph. As expected, stereotypical characteristics were assigned to mesomorphic and endomorphic silhouettes. Mesomorphic silhouettes were described as friendly, having the most friends, healthy, competent, aggressive, and likely to be a professional. Endomorphic silhouettes were described as being the sloppiest dresser, likely to have a menial job, depressed, and likely to conform to other's wishes. The responses assigned to ectomorphic silhouettes centered on their being concerned with appearance, knowledgeable about nutrition, sexually appealing, and dating often. Overall, female subjects indicated their desire to have an ectomorphic body build. Today's obsession with thinness in females clearly prevailed in the subjects' responses.

What we see in Keas and Beer's (1992) study, and in the previous study (Spillman & Everington, 1989), is that body type is capable of eliciting relatively common responses, at least from college students. But what responses might we expect from children ages 6 to 10 years old? Staffieri (1967) presented ninety 6- to 10-year-old subjects with silhouettes representing extreme somatotypes—endomorph, mesomorph, and ectomorph—and asked them to assign a series of behavior/personality trait adjectives to them. The results of Staffieri's research are displayed in Table 10.2, "Frequency of Assignment of Adjectives to Silhouettes by Subjects 6 to 10 Years Old." Staffieri's results parallel those of Keas and Beer: mesomorphs win hands down! Mesomorphs are described as strong, best friend, clean, happy, polite, honest, brave, good-looking, smart, and neat. Ectomorphs (thin) are described as quiet, worried, nervous, sick, sneaky, afraid, sad, and weak. Endomorphs (fat) are described as cheats, people who argue, lie, and get teased, and as lazy, dirty, and stupid. Staffieri concludes by stating that "the results of this study indicate a rather clear stereotype pattern for the three body images within age levels and across age levels. The mesomorph image is perceived as entirely favorable" (1967, p. 103).

**Table 10.2**
**Frequency of Assignment of Adjectives to Silhouettes**
**by Subjects 6 to 10 Years Old**

| Adjectives | Silhouettes | | |
|---|---|---|---|
| | En | M | Ec |
| Strong | 15 | 74 | 1 |
| Best friend | 9 | 67 | 14 |
| Quiet | 21 | 10 | 59 |
| Fights | 40 | 45 | 5 |
| Kind | 24 | 35 | 31 |
| Cheats | 63 | 9 | 18 |
| Clean | 3 | 54 | 33 |
| Worries | 30 | 11 | 49 |
| Lots of friends | 8 | 69 | 13 |
| Nervous | 42 | 5 | 43 |
| Happy | 19 | 54 | 17 |
| Help others | 17 | 55 | 18 |
| Polite | 13 | 50 | 27 |
| Argues | 58 | 17 | 15 |
| Remembers | 10 | 26 | 26 |
| Gets teased | 60 | 4 | 26 |
| Lonely | 33 | 9 | 48 |
| Sick | 41 | 7 | 42 |
| Forgets | 51 | 14 | 25 |
| Lazy | 67 | 5 | 18 |
| Healthy | 4 | 77 | 9 |
| Lies | 56 | 10 | 24 |
| Sneaky | 25 | 24 | 41 |

**Table 10.2 (Continued)**
**Frequency of Assignment of Adjectives to Silhouettes**
**by Subjects 6 to 10 Years Old**

| Adjectives | Silhouettes | | |
|---|---|---|---|
|  | **En** | **M** | **Ec** |
| Honest | 13 | 61 | 16 |
| Sloppy | 72 | 9 | 9 |
| Brave | 8 | 68 | 14 |
| Teases | 35 | 30 | 25 |
| Naughty | 46 | 18 | 26 |
| Good looking | 1 | 74 | 15 |
| Mean | 54 | 19 | 17 |
| Afraid | 27 | 7 | 56 |
| Ugly | 77 | 4 | 9 |
| Sad | 31 | 11 | 48 |
| Smart | 5 | 67 | 18 |
| Dirty | 60 | 16 | 14 |
| Tired | 39 | 12 | 39 |
| Stupid | 58 | 8 | 24 |
| Weak | 21 | 0 | 69 |
| Neat | 2 | 73 | 5 |

Although strangers' judgments (i.e., college student experimental subjects) might be easily influenced by others' body builds, one might expect that a mother's evaluation of her child in relationship to the child's body build would be immune from such superficial influences. Wrong! Walker (1963) designed a form on which parents could record a broad spectrum of temperament variables regarding their nursery-school-aged children. Independent judges evaluated 147 children's body builds using dimensions described by Sheldon (1940, 1954). Although not reaching levels of significance, "Two-thirds of the predictions made concerning the probable direction of association with each behavior item with each physique variable were confirmed" (p. 21).

Is one's self-concept a function of one's body build? According to Tucker (1984), the answer is yes. Tucker administered the Tennessee Self-Concept Scale, Eysenck Personality Inventory, Body Cathexis, and Perceived Somatotype Scale to 285 male college students. Males who reported a discrepancy between what they perceived their physiques to be and what they would like their body builds to be "displayed significantly more negative feelings toward abilities, worth, and satisfaction than did those who showed no such discrepancy" (p. 1232). They also "displayed characteristics of low self-concept, neuroticism, and body dissatisfaction significantly more than did those who expressed no self-ideal discrepancy" (p. 1233).

As you read this chapter, if you felt that you kept reading the same results over and over again—everyone favors mesomorphic body builds and everyone desires to have that particular physique—then this chapter has been worthwhile reading.

## TIME FOR INTROSPECTION—WHAT ARE YOUR EXPECTATIONS?

As a preservice or in-service teacher, what expectations do you or your colleagues form, if any, regarding students based upon their body build? If you or your colleagues don't form any, you are probably the exception. To what extent do you act on these expectations, that is, treat students differently based upon their body build?

All other things being equal, who would you most likely see cast as Romeo in an upcoming *Romeo and Juliet* play Joe—who (to be polite) could be described as "a bit portly," or Bill, who has a more typical high schooler's build? Who would you most likely see cast as Juliet—Carol, who has a significant "weight problem," or Rebecca, who, like Bill, has a more typical high schooler's slim build? Too often, Joe and Carol would be long-shot choices. After all, one might argue, Romeo and Juliet must look the part of young lovers and, well, bite my tongue, how can two significantly overweight teenagers be Shakespearean lovers?

Look back over your high school yearbooks and see who was selected as king and queen for the prom? Chances are very high that the king had a mesomorphic (average) body build and the queen had a mesomorphic (average) or ectomorphic (thin) body build. Coincidence? Perhaps, perhaps not.

Who do you most often select to lead a group, to demonstrate something in front of the entire class, or to put something important on the chalkboard? Would you say that you evenly distribute these tasks around the room without ever taking students' body builds into consideration? If the answer is yes, good for you. If the answer is no, then do something about it.

# CHAPTER 11

# SOCIOECONOMIC LEVELS
# AND THE SFP

## INTRODUCTION

When you are at the grocery store checkout counter waiting in line and observe someone in front of you "paying" for his or her order with government-supplied food stamps and you are paying with cold, hard cash, what thoughts go through your mind? Do you have a tendency to size up this person negatively and wonder why the individual doesn't get a job and pay their own way just like everyone else—just like you? Or, do you give the person the benefit of the doubt and simply thank God (or someone) that you don't need such government help?

Perhaps your judgments, in other words, your expectations, are influenced by what "60 Minutes," "Date Line," or "20/20" exposé was on the television the night before. Perhaps your expectations are influenced by whether you are a conservative or a liberal. No matter what influenced your expectations, different people will have different expectations and, as predicted by the self-fulfilling prophecy, will exhibit differential behaviors.

Americans are becoming more and more polarized. It can be argued that this polarization can be attributed much more to the fact that we have created an ever-widening socioeconomic gulf between the haves and the have-nots, than to any differences in our skin color or ethnicity. The have-nots are envious and distrustful of the haves, while the haves are threatened by and show disdain for the have-nots. Further, the haves wonder why the have-nots don't simply stop taking government handouts, stop complaining, and start working harder so they, too, or at least their children, can make it into the haves group.

In schools, the haves and the have-nots are easily identified. Cumulative record files and other student records reveal which students live on which "side of the tracks," which students qualify for free or reduced-price breakfast and lunch programs, and which students come from single-parent homes. The students themselves advertise their socioeconomic status in the clothes they wear, the jewelry they adorn themselves with, and the sheen to their hair. Even in nonpublic schools where the students wear uniforms, the haves and the have-nots are known by everyone, including teachers. Like their public school counterparts, nonpublic school teachers are influenced (form expectations) based on these socioeconomic differences.

My wife and I made a conscious effort to take advantage of the fact that teachers are predisposed to expect more of students of higher socioeconomic levels. For the first day of school, we made sure that David and Rebecca were "bright-eyed and bushy-tailed." Their hair was recently cut, they had new school clothes and school supplies (i.e., book bag, notebooks, pens, calculator), they were scrubbed well, their fingernails were clean, and their teeth were brushed.

We made it a point to attend each and every parent's night for David and Rebecca and, without sounding too high and mighty, let it be known that I had a Ph.D. and taught at a major university and that my wife had an M.A. and was the head of the English Department at a local high school. It was also known that David and Rebecca accompanied my wife and me on sabbatical for a year in England and 6-months in Australia, and at other times had traveled to Great Britain, France, the Netherlands, West Germany, East Germany (including Berlin before the wall came down), New Zealand, Greece, Canada, and Mexico. All of this added up to, at least in the minds of David's and Rebecca's teachers, our having an above-average socioeconomic status.

## WHAT THE SFP RESEARCH HAS TO SAY

In a study by Michlin (1977), 56 preservice English teachers read personal information about student writers and then read their essays. It appears as if lower social-status students have the advantage, because teachers rated their essays higher than other students' essays. What at first glance seems to be an advantage, though, really may be the teachers' lower expectations of these lower social-status students. In fact, when the same essays were believed to have been written by higher status students the essays were rated lower. Could it be that the teachers, in their hearts, knew (i.e., expected) that these higher social-status students could do better?

Social status in a community can be viewed a number of ways. Sometimes, family structure (whether one is from a divorced or an intact family) conveys social status. Delcampo (1983) had 60 female undergraduate college students majoring in preschool teacher education, divided into two groups of 30, view videotapes of a preschool boy and a preschool girl. One group was told that the boy and girl in the tapes were from a divorced family, and the other group was told that the children were from an intact family. After viewing the videotapes, subjects were asked to rate the children on a Personality Trait Rating Scale and a Predicted Behavior in School Scale. The reviewers "rated divorced home children significantly lower than intact children on personality traits and predicted school behaviors" (p. 379). The implications for children entering school is clear. Their family status (i.e., divorced or intact) can trigger expectations for which, according to self-fulfilling prophecy theory, teachers are only too willing to seek verifying evidence.

Although teachers may not know a lot about their incoming students, especially those entering preschool programs such as Head Start, they often do learn something about students' parents from available records. A study by Thornton (1984), where 160 Head Start teachers read descriptions of a Head Start child's home environment (i.e., race of child, intactness of parents' marriage), "suggests that characteristics of the parents were more influential in teachers' ratings than were child characteristics" (p. 2814). Therefore, even before the teacher meets the incoming Head Start child, expectations have been formed.

Sometimes teachers' expectations of students are formed not by who the students are as individuals but, instead, by the mere fact that the students are seen to be part of a larger group. The expectations, then, that are held for the larger group extend to the individual students. Price (1985) conducted a study with fifth-grade teachers from Detroit who evaluated similar work samples from fifth-grade students believed to be attending one of two types of schools—high achieving or low achieving. Among the major findings was that "there is a significant difference in the level of achievement expected by teachers in high achieving schools compared to teachers in low achieving schools" (p. 3248). For those parents who can afford it, it may be wise to move into a school district where their child could attend a high-achieving school. The expectations of the school's high achievement should, via the teachers, rub off on the student body.

A review of the literature by Cooper (1989) supports the fact that not only do teachers' expectations of student performance influence student achievement, an overall theme of this book, but "teacher expectations of students' performance may vary as a function of students' social class" (p. 1763). Low-socioeconomic-status students are at risk, according to Cooper. Brantlinger (1994), too, claims that the socioeconomic status of low-income students (as opposed to high-income students) were found to be very aware of their teachers' attitudes toward them.

In a questionnaire-based study, Boyce (1990) asked suburban primary school teachers to predict the academic success of their students through the rest of the year, through high school, and through college. The teachers were divided into three groups—those who taught high SES (socioeconomic status) students, those who taught average SES students, and those who taught low SES students but had received specific training in how to do so. The investigator concluded that "this study supported current literature indicating that teachers in high SES schools had higher or greater expectations for student academic achievement than did their counterparts in low SES schools" (p. 1981). Unfortunately, having received training in how to teach low SES students did not appear to make any difference.

Do students of differing socioeconomic levels pick up on teachers' differential expectations and the differential behaviors that follow? According to Brantlinger (1994), "social class turned out to be a potent force in the adolescents' thinking" (p. 192) regarding teachers' expectations. Lower income students felt that teachers disliked them personally and favored students from higher-income families. Higher income students, on the other hand, took it for granted that teachers liked them.

Although this chapter is relatively short in comparison to some others, this should not be interpreted as meaning that the socioeconomic status of students is any less important as a basis for teachers forming expectations of students. In fact, socioeconomic status often can be correlated with other factors such as race and ethnicity—that is, many minorities are also economically disadvantaged. Whether it is a student's social class, race, ethnicity, or some combination of these factors that triggers teachers' expectations, the potential for real damage exists. Given that teachers often are of a different social class, race, or ethnicity from that of their students, it is doubly important that teachers are aware of the preconceived stereotypes that they may bring into their classrooms.

## A TIME FOR INTROSPECTION—WHAT ARE YOUR EXPECTATIONS?

As a preservice or in-service teacher, what expectations do you or your colleagues form, if any, regarding students based upon their socioeconomic level? If you or your colleagues don't form any, you are probably the exception. To what extent do you act on these expectations, that is, treat students differently based upon their socioeconomic level?

How much of your behavior toward students is based upon your knowledge of which "side of the tracks" they come from—Pill Hill, where all the doctors live, or Harrison Village, the primarily black housing project near the river? Do students' clothes and their conditions, that is, whether they're clean, recently pressed, trendy, all signs of higher or lower socioeconomic status, influence how you act toward students? If you have ever substitute taught, did you just know (i.e., were you able to predict) what you were getting yourself in for when you substituted in an affluent suburban school and what you were getting yourself in for when you substituted in one of the inner-city schools? How often were you right? Did you dress differently when you taught at the two schools? Did you anticipate having to discipline differently (i.e., with respect to frequency, harshness, etc.) when you taught at the two schools? Could it be that your expectations, conveyed through your differential behaviors, helped these expectations come true?

When formally or informally counseling students regarding their future career choices, do you tend to see some students as more likely being successful in a vocational-technical career and other students as more likely being successful in a professional or managerial career? Is there any correlation between what you see as reasonable career paths for students and what you know about the students' socioeconomic level?

Higher socioeconomic status often buys students greater teacher and peer attention. For instance, whether it is asking elementary school students to recall what they did on their summer vacation or asking high school students how they plan to spend their upcoming Christmas vacation, chances are that higher socioeconomic-level children will have more interesting and exciting responses—they traveled to Sanabel Island in Florida; went to Williamsburg, Virginia; or will be going to Vale, Colorado, to ski or to St. Johns in the British Virgin Islands to sail. In comparison, what can the lower socioeconomic-level child, who plans to spend the summer playing in the city streets, have to say that will be as interesting?

As just one personal example, my wife and two children (David and Rebecca) joined me for my year's sabbatical at Durham University in northern England and, later, for my 6-month sabbatical at the University of Melbourne in Australia. In both cases, my children went to school in these countries, and they traveled extensively in Great Britain, France, Germany, Australia, and New Zealand. My socioeconomic status (college professor) gave our children a rare opportunity that lower socioeconomic-status children likely do not enjoy. Each time our children returned home and started back to school, their experiences made them the center of attention in the eyes of both teachers and fellow students. Would your expectations of David and Rebecca have been influenced? Perhaps!

# CHAPTER 12

# SPECIAL NEEDS STUDENTS AND THE SFP

## INTRODUCTION

What do teachers expect of special needs students? Until Public Law 94-142, the Education for All Handicapped Children Act of 1975, was passed, few teachers other than special education teachers thought much about special needs children, one way or the other. Prior to this piece of legislation, even if the vast majority of non–special education teachers held erroneous negative expectations for these special needs children, little damage was done. These children were someone else's problem. Now, with special needs children being mainstreamed into the "least restrictive environments," new as well as seasoned regular classroom teachers are being required to participate in writing individualized education programs (IEPs) for their students and then implementing these programs. All of a sudden, every teacher's expectations of special needs children are crucial.

A new vocabulary exploded on the scene to describe the categories of special needs children—learning disabled, emotionally disturbed, physically handicapped, mentally retarded, trainable, and gifted. Surely one common element contributing to success in teaching children in each of these categories is that teachers possess appropriately high, positive expectations for them. Just like the children's story *The Little Engine That Could*, teachers who go into a classroom of special needs children believing "I know he can, I know he can, I know he can" are more likely, like the "little engine that could," together with the children, to make it to the top!

What is unfortunate is that many teacher-preparation institutions still do not require a course dealing with the needs of special children—especially for secondary-level content teachers. The result is that too many teachers enter the classroom and come in contact with special needs students for the first time having only preconceived notions (often negative) about what these children are capable of achieving.

## WHAT THE SFP RESEARCH HAS TO SAY

Labels such as "educable mentally retarded" do appear to influence the expectations of teachers. Aloia and MacMillan (1983), using a 54-item questionnaire, surveyed the initial expectations that 114 regular-classroom elementary teachers held for handicapped children who were about to be mainstreamed. The teachers were provided with a photograph and some background data, including a special education label (in this case, EMR), for each child. The presence of the EMR label proved to be a significant influence on the teachers' expectations regarding students' academic ability. Further, the negative impact of the EMR label was greater when the child in question also was judged as average in attractiveness.

In a similar study using both special education resource teachers and regular teachers as evaluators, Aloia and Aloia (1982) found that regular teachers who examined children's cumulative record folders had lower expectations for the handicapped children than did the special education teachers. If these lower expectations accompany the children into mainstreamed regular classrooms, the self-fulfilling prophecy likely will work against these students.

Labels such as "mentally retarded" do influence teachers' expectations, at least preservice teachers' expectations, of special needs students. Foil (1980) found that even in the face of evidence to the contrary, for example, through tutoring students who were not actually mentally retarded, preservice teachers held lower expectations of students they were led to believe were mentally retarded. Similar results were found by Carter (1981). In this study teacher expectations had more of an effect on teachers' behaviors toward special needs students than did the reality of the students' behavior.

All students, including special needs children, should be challenged. Teachers who hold low expectations of special needs children are ill prepared to offer this needed challenge. Although no one would advocate expecting more from special needs children than they are able to produce, at the same time one should not expect less from them than they are able to produce. "Once students' current skill levels are obtained, teacher expectations should be realistic and demanding enough to cause them to strive for optimum achievement" (Glazzard, 1984, p. 139).

No special needs students, including those who are hearing impaired, appear to be immune from the negative impact of the self-fulfilling prophecy. According to Schleper (1995), setting low standards and expectations for the language achievement of students with hearing impairments, including deafness, results in a self-fulfilling prophecy. Teaching methods, instead, should stress high expectations and recognize differences among students as factors that can add richness to the exploration of language.

Do vocational-technical teachers hold different expectations for special needs students than do academic teachers? After all, the vocational-technical world is a more hands-on, concrete world of learning compared to the more theoretical, often abstract, academic world of most senior high schools. Unfortunately,

Frizzell (1986), using a Vocational Educators Expectation and Attitude Survey, found that vocational trade instructors, too, hold negative expectations of special needs students—i.e., those labeled "learning disabled," "emotionally retarded," "mentally retarded," and "orthopedically impaired."

Perhaps university teachers, in most cases possessing greater educational credentials than their basic-education counterparts, can see beyond a child's special needs label. Not so, argue Minner and Prater (1984). In their study, 210 faculty members from three midwestern universities were provided with brief, hypothetical academic and social characteristics vignettes—either positive or negative—on students who were thinking about scheduling the professor's class. Each university teacher completed an attitude questionnaire. Analyses of the questionnaires revealed that university faculty had the lowest expectations for students whose vignettes identified them as being learning disabled (LD). Not only were the teachers' outwardly directed expectations lower for LD-labeled students, but the faculty perceived (expected) themselves to be less able to teach such students successfully. "The LD label significantly and negatively influenced faculty members' initial expectations" (Minner & Prater, 1984, p. 228).

With the variety of special needs children's labels (i.e., LD, physically handicapped), the question is no longer so simple as asking whether teachers hold positive or negative expectations for special needs students. One must ask instead whether one holds positive or negative expectations for a particular category (label) of special needs students. Teachers' expectations may vary from label to label, or at least so say Rolison and Medway (1985).

In Rolison and Medway's (1985) study, 180 teachers who had at least two years of teaching experience in regular elementary school classrooms were asked to evaluate booklets that provided varying information about a hypothetical student. Unknown to the subjects, the information included in the booklets was altered in a number of ways, including occasionally labeling the student as learning disabled, or LD. Subjects were asked to predict whether the student would exceed the school district's academic average. The results of this study show that "actual classroom teachers raise or lower their expectations according to a student's previous special education label" (p. 569). Teachers were found to have higher expectations for students labeled "LD" than for those labeled "mildly retarded" (i.e., EMR).

Koster (1987) also confirmed that teachers hold different sets of expectations for different categories of special needs students. This researcher found that teachers' academic expectations of students were significantly higher for students labeled "average and physically handicapped" than for students labeled "mentally retarded," "learning disabled," and "emotionally disturbed." Teachers' behavioral expectations were significantly higher for children labeled "average," "physically handicapped," "mentally retarded," and "learning disturbed" than for children labeled "emotionally disturbed."

A very common situation is to have several children from the same family, only one of whom is a special needs student, enrolled in the same school or school district.  To what degree do the expectations teachers hold for special needs students also hold for those students' siblings?  In their investigation, Richey and Yesseldyke (1983) had 18 midwestern teachers (Grades K-5) from four school districts rate 27 younger siblings of LD and non-LD students. Results "indicted that teachers held lower expectations for younger siblings of LD than for non-LD students they were currently teaching" (p. 610). Specifically, siblings of LD students were expected to perform less well in reading, general knowledge, visual perception, and memory.  Of note is the fact that 72% of the teachers believed that the major cause of learning disability was environment—something, of course, that siblings share.

Thus far, the research cited for special needs students has ignored the category—the label—"gifted student."  Surely, the label "gifted" would create positive expectations in the minds of most educators, prompting them to behave in a manner conducive to gifted students' benefit.  This is not necessarily so. Research shows that there may be a negative side to the teacher expectations that accompany the "gifted student" label.

For instance, Kolb and Jussim (1994, p. 28), in citing the works of others, claim that "teachers expect gifted students to be alert, creative, eager, confident, composed, serious, and mature (Hall, 1983).  Additionally, gifted students are expected to be witty, enthusiastic (Bell & Roach, 1986), and highly motivated toward attaining goals (Freeman, 1983; Kramer, 1986).  Finally, people believe that gifted children will continuously strive for perfection in the work they perform inside and outside of school (Freeman, 1983)."

What happens when gifted students do not live up to these almost impossible expectations?  When gifted students do not perform academically up to their teachers' very high expectations, these teachers may lower their expectations and, more important, begin to treat the gifted students as underachievers.  If students can resist this low-achiever treatment and go on to change their teachers' perceptions, little damage may be done.  But, if so-called underachieving gifted students do not resist, or are unsuccessful in changing teachers' expectations, these students may well "deteriorate in a downward spiral" (Kolb & Jussim, 1994, p. 28).

There is no doubt that educators can be influenced by the special needs labels students carry with them.  Does it matter, though, how student assessment results are displayed to teachers?  Linehan, Brady, and Hwang (1991) say yes.  In their study they used 84 educators who had had instructional experience with students with severe disabilities.  The educators were divided into two groups—one provided with ecological assessment reports and one provided with development assessment reports.  An ecological assessment documented students' observed competencies in their daily environment; a developmental assessment reported mental and developmental ages determined through standardized testing. Educators were then asked to rate students' achievement on an Individualized Education Program (IEP) Questionnaire.  "Data analysis indicated that educators reading the ecological reports had significantly higher expectations for student accomplishment of IEP objectives than educators reading developmental reports" (p. 150). It appears, then, that assessment formats are linked to educators' expectations of students. Because expectations can influence subsequent instruction, and thus student achievement, care should be exercised in deciding upon assessment reporting formats.

As the steps in the self-fulfilling prophecy tell us, teachers' attitudes as to how to accommodate special needs students are colored by the initial expectations that teachers hold for these children. Public Law 94-142 or no public law, many regular (non–special education) teachers still may not be comfortable nor feel competent in mainstreaming special needs children. Willingness to mainstream special needs children often is based upon the teachers having had educational experiences designed to prepare them for mainstreaming (Stewart, 1993). Such educational experiences help regular teachers develop more positive and realistic expectations for these children.

Specifically, what characteristics of regular classroom teachers make them more likely to accept handicapped students into their classrooms? Stewart (1993), using 167 teachers who taught kindergarten through third grade, investigated seven variables that were thought to influence these teachers' willingness to mainstream special needs students. Two of the seven variables—having had experiences that prepared them for mainstreaming and believing that mainstreamed handicapped students are not disruptive enough to hinder overall teacher effectiveness—were found to relate to teachers' willingness to integrate special needs students.

So far, the expectations research reported primarily has concentrated upon just one end of the special children continuum—that is, LD, EMR, and handicapped students. One might expect, and in fact one has seen, that teachers hold lower expectations for these children than they hold for regular children. What impact do teachers' expectations have on students from the other end of the special children continuum—that is, gifted students?

What happens to student motivation when students designated as gifted are placed in classrooms with their intellectual peers? Clinkenbeard (1991) investigated this situation by studying 14 sixth graders who had been identified as being cognitively gifted. These fourteen students were placed together in combined reading and language arts classes for two class periods each day. They then spent the rest of the day in regular classes with other students.

When surveyed about their impression as to what was expected of them by peers and teachers, gifted students felt, among other things, that when they were placed in groups with regular students that they ended up doing all the work (for which others took all the credit), that non-gifted students believed that gifted students did not have to study hard to get good grades, and that it was next to impossible to meet the high academic and behavioral expectations held for them by teachers. In fact, gifted students felt that teachers graded their work harder than they graded non-gifted students' work. In summary, the gifted students stated that "regular classroom teachers and peers have unfair expectations for gifted students" (p. 61).

## A TIME FOR INTROSPECTION—WHAT ARE YOUR EXPECTATIONS?

As a preservice or in-service teacher, what expectations do you or your colleagues form, if any, regarding students based upon their special needs status? If you or your colleagues don't form any, you are probably the exception. To what extent do you act on these expectations, that is, treat students differently based upon their special needs status?

Given that most classroom teachers have little or no training in how to diagnose and work with special needs students, it is little wonder that teachers' expectations vary from expecting far too little to expecting far too much from students. Expectations, to be useful, should be high, yet reasonable. Without training, how are teachers supposed to know what is reasonable to expect? What is reasonable to expect from an LD (learning disabled) student, an EMR (emotionally mentally retarded) student, a wheelchair-bound student, a gifted student?

What are your expectations of these special needs students? How much are your expectations, and therefore your behaviors, influenced by the labels students are assigned? Do you catch yourself expecting LD students to know less and therefore asking them easier questions in class? How much easier? Do you believe that the label LD means some form of mental retardation? Do you discipline EMR students less frequently and less harshly, believing (i.e., expecting) that they "just can't help themselves"? Do you do things for wheelchair-bound students that you would not do for nonwheelchair-bound students? Could it be that your actions toward special needs students are governed by your expectations (often unproven) regarding their capabilities?

One final caution regarding forming expectations about special needs children. Certainly a teacher should not form expectations of children's ability and/or behavior *simply* upon the basis of their special needs labels. Data, not labels, should be our basis for forming expectations. Unfortunately, data gathered from many commonly administered school-based instruments, such as written tests, inventories, performance measures, anecdotal records, and so forth, can be totally useless unless there is evidence that these measurements both are reliable and valid. Without the presence of these two crucial factors—reliability and validity—the data used by teacher decision makers is of little or no real value!

# CHAPTER 13

# THE SFP FROM THE STUDENTS' SIDE OF THE DESK

## INTRODUCTION

According to Jean Piaget, when we were young children, we were egocentric. We believed that how we saw things was how everyone saw them. Further, we thought that we were the only ones doing the judging—forming the expectations. As we matured, we learned that everyone does not view the world as we do and that others are judging us just as much as we judge them. It was really scary to learn for the first time that others had been forming expectations of us just as often as we had been forming expectations of them. Judgment—the basis of expectation—then, is a two-way street.

In classrooms, not only do teachers form expectations of students and consequently behave toward them in a manner consistent with those expectations, but students too form expectations of teachers and then act on them. The result is that not only are teachers in a position to wield the SFP and impact the lives (i.e., achievement, motivation, performance) of students, but students themselves are using the same SFP process to impact the lives of teachers. Because the SFP is being wielded by both sides, no one, neither the teacher nor the student, is completely the master of his or her fate. The sooner teachers realize this, the better off they will be. Unfortunately, there is little research examining the effect of student expectations on teachers.

In any school, at any grade level, information about teachers, such as whether they are competent, demanding, strict, or caring and whether they return assignments quickly, correct for grammar, and permit tardiness, quickly travels the students' informal grapevine. Some schools, in fact, formally publish information about individual teachers so that students can learn ahead of time what to expect from Mr. or Mrs. So-and-so or from such-and-such course. In other words, students use this information—a form of first impressions—valid or not, to form expectations about teachers and courses they are about to take

**Figure 13.1**
**Students Sizing Up This Year's Teacher**

If this picture looks suspiciously like Figure 3.1,
"Teacher Sizing Up This Year's Students," it should.
Both teachers and students 'size up' each other.

(Figure 13.1). Many teachers, especially seasoned teachers, use these expectations to their advantage. They have taught long enough to develop a "reputation." Everyone knows that if you take Mr. So-and-so's class, he will work your tail off, or if you schedule a class with Mrs. Such-and-such, she will put up with no monkey business whatsoever. Pity the teacher, though, who has earned a less-than-favorable reputation regarding his or her subject matter competence or classroom control.

## WHAT THE SFP RESEARCH HAS TO SAY

A study by Feldman and Prohaska (1979) titled "The Student as Pygmalion: Effect of Student Expectation on the Teacher" demonstrated how teachers' attitudes and behaviors can be affected by students' expectations. Clearly, students can be Pygmalions for teachers. In Experiment 1 of their study, Feldman and Prohaska told 39 female undergraduates in an introductory psychology class that they were going to be taught by and then evaluate a third-year student teacher in education. While waiting to be taught, the subjects, one at a time, sat in a hallway where an experimenter confederate was filling out an evaluation questionnaire as if he had just observed the student teacher teaching. The confederate orally offered his evaluation (predetermined to create either a positive or negative expectation) of the student teacher and, under the pretense of having to leave in a hurry, left his evaluation questionnaire with the subject, asking her to turn it in. The subject was left in the hallway for a period of time sufficient for her to read the confederate's evaluation.

The student teacher, also an experimenter confederate, was trained to deliver the lesson in the same manner each time. After watching the student teacher teach, each subject was asked to complete her own evaluation questionnaire. The subjects, depending upon their experimental manipulation, responded quite differently. Subjects expecting the student teacher to do a poor job rated the lesson as being more difficult and less interesting and judged the teacher to be less competent, intelligent, and enthusiastic. The exact opposite was true for those expecting the student teacher to do a good job.

Experiment 1 showed that subjects' expectations can and do influence their evaluations. How do subjects, once their high or low expectations have been formed, convey their expectations? In Experiment 2, Feldman and Prohaska (1979) used 43 undergraduate female students who, for extra credit in an introductory psychology course, taught other undergraduates (two at a time) a brief lesson. Unknown to the teachers, the two undergraduates playing the role of students were experimenter confederates. These confederates were trained to use either positive nonverbal behaviors (i.e., leaning forward, sitting closer to and being directly oriented toward, and gazing at the teacher 50% of the time) or negative nonverbal behaviors (leaning back, sitting further from and shoulders turned away from, and gazing at the teacher 10% of the time). Each confederate correctly answered 8 of 10 questions asked by the teacher.

At the end of each teaching session, teacher subjects were asked to complete a questionnaire evaluating attitudinal, nonverbal, and performance measures. Teacher subjects who had students who exhibited positive nonverbal behaviors felt happier, warmer, and more competent than did teacher subjects who had students who exhibited negative nonverbal behaviors. A 20-second sample from each teacher subject's teaching was videotaped and shown to two untrained judges. When asked, "What is the overall adequacy of the teacher's performance?" the judges more often rated the teacher subjects supplied with positive nonverbal behavior as "very adequate" than they did the teacher subjects supplied with negative nonverbal behavior. Clearly, "neither teachers nor students are the sole Pygmalion in the classroom" (p. 492).

What happens when both the teacher's and the students' expectations regarding each other are manipulated, and then the two are put together? Feldman and Theiss (1982) did just this. In their study, "sixty subjects were designated as teachers and were led to expect either a high- or low-ability student, whereas sixty subjects, acting as students, were independently led to expect either a high- or low-competent teacher" (p. 217). The two were then paired in a randomly assigned teaching situation. Following the teaching session, both performance and attitudinal measures were administered. The results showed that students performed better when the teacher had high expectations of them and that the students viewed the lesson more positively if they had expected the teacher to be competent. Teachers' behavior, too, was affected by the expectations they held for students. Independent judges evaluating 20-second teaching samples noted a difference in how competent teachers appeared. In conclusion, "Support was found for the notion that both the expectations of the teacher and student do have an effect on the outcome and feelings of success of both partners in the dyad" (p. 222).

In an experiment similar to the one above, Zanna, Sheras, and Cooper (1975) used junior high school students taking part in a summer enrichment program in English and math as subjects. In the study, "teachers were given positive expectancies about the potential of half of the students and no expectancies regarding the other half. In addition, half of the students in each of these groups were told that they would probably perform well in the program while half were given no such expectations" (p. 279). Students' performance in English and math was measured via a pretest and posttest.

Of little surprise to the reader is the fact that students who were led to believe that they would perform well in fact did perform better than students who had been given no such positive self-expectations. Thus, even in the absence of any positive teacher expectancy, students who were told they would perform well fulfilled their own expectations. Further, students whose teachers were told they would perform well did perform well, even in the absence of the students' own positive self-expectations. The unexpected outcome of this study came when student performance was measured for the desirable combination of both positive student self-expectations and positive teacher expectations. The surprise was that no improvement whatsoever occurred for this group! Can expectations be too high and thus cause frustration and anxiety on both the student's and teacher's part? The authors hypothesize just such an explanation for this unexpected outcome.

Rappaport and Rappaport (1975), in an article titled "The Other Half of the Expectancy Equation: Pygmalion," reinforce the fact that any equation, even a "human" equation, has two sides. On one side, we have the teacher and his or her expectations of students. On the other side, we have the students and their expectations of themselves. In their study, Rappaport and Rappaport (1975) used several groups, including, among others: (1) a Teacher Expectancy (TE) group of three teachers who were supplied with very positive information about less frequently and less harshly selected students they were about to have in their class—for example, statements that the students were highly motivated and had high potential, and (2) a Pupil Expectancy (PE) group of 45 urban black school children, ages 5 and 6, who, prior to meeting their regular teachers, were praised for their superior performance and made to feel that they had exceptional talent.

In effect, the first group, the TEs, represented the traditional self-fulfilling prophecy design of manipulating the expectations of the teacher. The second group, the PEs, represented an effort to induce positive expectations directly into the minds of students regarding their own talent and potential. A subsequent 12-week instructional period followed where students, both those led to believe they had potential and talent and those who acted as a control, and teachers worked together. Teachers were unaware of the fact that some students' expectations of themselves had been manipulated. After the instructional period, a test designed to measure reading achievement was administered. The researchers found that "inducing positive expectations in the pupils was more effective than the conventional teacher manipulation. It was concluded that the focus of educational programs should be the potentially malleable child rather than the sometimes intransigent teacher" (Rappaport & Rappaport, 1975, p. 531).

In addition to the fact that most students form expectations of teachers, some students have figured out how to manipulate the teacher's expectations of them (students). In an article titled "Lowered Expectations: How Schools Reward Incompetence," Jackson (1985) notes that students who "play dumb" can earn easier classes, lower expectations, reduced pressure, and individual attention. Truly, here is the potential for the "inmates running the prison."

## A TIME FOR INTROSPECTION—WHAT ARE YOUR EXPECTATIONS?

Now that you know that you are the target of students' expectations—well, perhaps this is enough said!

# CHAPTER 14

# PRESERVICE AND IN-SERVICE SFP TRAINING

## INTRODUCTION

What can teachers, administrators, parents, and others, including students themselves, do to control the SFP? Slightly tongue-in-cheek, I offer Remedy 1. On a more practical note, at least as it applies to one's given or surname, I offer Remedy 2. The real answer, though, lies in Remedy 3, conducting preservice and in-service training programs designed to help participants understand how the self-fulfilling prophecy works and how it can be controlled.

## REMEDY 1: HANDICAPPING

Maybe we could provide some sort of a golf-type handicap point system for students in order to create a level playing field. If what should count in evaluating a student's achievement is what is between his or her ears—what the student knows about the subject matter—and yet, what actually counts, as much or more, is the student's gender, race, ethnicity, weight, attractiveness, body build, socioeconomic status, and surname, then the playing field is not level.

Perhaps fat kids and skinny kids, kids with strange names, and kids who come from single parent families dependent on welfare, for example, should be given a handicap—extra points, some form of statistical advantage. Awarding such points would not be a gift, giving them an advantage. Quite the contrary. These awarded extra points would simply be a recognition of how unfairly some students are being treated based upon personal characteristics that should not, but do influence a teacher's evaluation. Goebel and Cashen (1979), in fact, recommend that "a rigorous effort should be made to identify those biases present and to use appropriate statistical procedures to control for them" (p. 652).

If we don't do something, and what is suggested above may not be the ideal "something," then ideal-weight children with desirable names who are attractive and come from two-parent professional families, and so forth will receive higher evaluations than they deserve, while other children will receive lower evaluations than they deserve—all because of factors that have little or nothing to do with the student performance being evaluated.

Teachers, too, would qualify for evaluation handicaps. I suppose that teachers who are too thin or too heavy, too young or too old, too tall or too short, too good looking or too ugly, too masculine or too feminine, and so forth would all be entitled to handicap points in order to make their playing field level. It remains to be seen how many teachers would actually initiate the actions required for them to apply for, and document, their state of being too much this and too much that.

## REMEDY 2: CHANGING WHAT YOU CAN CHANGE

A better remedy than that of creating a golf-type handicap point system would be to educate people, especially parents, teachers, and students, about how expectations are formed and how these expectations can then influence our behaviors. Actually, this suggestion is the whole point of this book.

For instance, although we cannot do much about our gender, race, stature, ethnicity, and ability, we can do something about our names. Here we can make a real difference if we are tuned into the world's expectations regarding names. Yet, it could be argued that parents spend about as much time figuring out what to name a family pet (Fido, Spot, Ginger, Butch) as they do deciding what to name a newborn child.

If, due to your parents' lack of forethought, you are saddled with an unpopular name, then you can correct the situation by changing it. Note, many movie and rock stars have done just this. John Wayne's real name was Marion Michael Morrison. Which name, John Wayne or Marion Morrison, best fits with this famous movie star's *True Grit* image? Which name, Marilyn Monroe or Norma Jean Mortenson, best fits a blond bombshell calendar and movie star? They are, of course, one and the same person.

The examples go on and on. The Beatles' drummer Ringo Starr was born Richard Starkey, the rock star Stevie Wonder was born Steveland Morris Hardaway; television and movie star Stefanie Powers was born Stefania Zofia Federkiewicz; James Garner, the *Rockford Files* television series star, was born James Baumgardner; movie star Kirk Douglas was born Issur Danielovitch (Michael, Kirk's actor son, surely appreciates the name change); and comedian/writer Woody Allen was born Allen Stewart Konigsberg. Of note is the fact that on the way up the ladder to stardom, Sylvester Stallone, as he is now known, used the name Sly Stallone. He is now powerful enough in the movie industry to use his less-than-macho given name Sylvester without any fear of repercussions.

If there is reason to believe that your given name actually generates negative expectations in the minds of others, instead of changing it altogether, consider using your initials in place of your first and/or middle names. In education and psychology, everyone recognizes the famous behaviorist B. F. Skinner. How many, though, recognize him as Burrhus Frederic Skinner? Other examples of famous individuals who have chosen to use initials are A. S. Neill (of *Summerhill* fame), William F. Buckley (columnist and editor of *The Atlantic Monthly*), O. J. Simpson (football hero and, more recently, defendant), and Harry S. Truman (president who claimed to have no middle name but just added the letter *S*). If they can do it, so can you.

Companies, too, recognize the power of initials in a name. When E. F. Hutton (financial advisor) speaks, at least in the television commercial, everyone listens. Everyone recognizes the names J. C. Penney and H. J. Heinz, but few can tell you what the initials stand for.

## REMEDY 3: PRESERVICE AND IN-SERVICE TRAINING

When the self-fulfilling prophecy is brought to their attention, most teachers immediately see both its positive and its negative sides. Although teachers know in their heart that they should look for the good in students and avoid using negative labels (Metcalf, 1995), in practice they often seem to do just the opposite. In the same way, most of us know in our heart that we should consume less fat, eat less red meat, and exercise more, but in practice we violate these intentions.

When teachers believe that they can influence student learning, they usually do. "The Power of Believing," the title of an article by Weber and Omotani (1994), points out how important it is for teachers to hold positive expectations of students. Teacher expectancy effects, especially negative effects, are most evident when teachers are unaware of the possibility of such effects (Smith & Luginbuhl, 1976). Hence, what teachers need is a well-designed preservice and/or in-service program that introduces them to the self-fulfilling prophecy and regularly reinforces this knowledge over time. Hassenpflug (1994), like other successful classroom teachers, holds the belief that student achievement and attitude can improve dramatically as a result of high teacher expectations.

### Teacher Expectations of Student Achievement (TESA)—A Training Program

One such popular SFP training program is the Phi Delta Kappa–supported TESA (Teacher Expectations and Student Achievement) interaction model developed by the Los Angeles County Office of Education. The TESA project was inspired by early studies on teacher expectations conducted by Thomas Good and Jere Brophy (cited in this book).

The TESA interaction model (Table 14.1) consists of five monthly workshops, each of which addresses three strands—Response Opportunities, Feedback, and Personal Regard. In all, 15 separate teacher-student interactions are stressed.   In each of these workshops, fundamental differences in how teachers treat students, differences based upon the teachers' expectations of them, are explored.   This training enables teachers to "confront their expectations of student performance objectively and learn to alter inaccurate expectations" (Patriarca & Kragt, 1986, p. 50).

**Table 14.1**
**TESA INTERACTION MODEL**

| MONTHLY WORKSHOPS | STRAND<br>Response Opportunities | STRAND<br>Feedback | STRAND<br>Personal Regard |
|---|---|---|---|
| 1 | Equitable Distribution | Affirm/Correct | Proximity |
| 2 | Individual Help | Praise | Courtesy |
| 3 | Latency | Reasons for Praise | Personal Interest and Compliments |
| 4 | Delving | Listening | Touching |
| 5 | Higher-Level Questioning | Accepting Feelings | Desist |

Source: Page A-2, the "TESA Interaction Model," of the *TESA Teacher's Manual*, is used with permission of the Los Angeles County Office of Education, TESA development, publication, and training (Phone: 1-800-566-6651 or 1-310-922-6111).[1]

For instance, in the TESA model, "courtesy" is defined as an example of the Personal Regard strand.   Therefore, "if the attention a student receives from the teacher is considered a demonstration of courtesy, many females and minorities are treated discourteously" (*TESA*, 1993, p. D-23).   This fact, along with its ramifications for student achievement, is presented to TESA participants.

As another instance, the TESA model defines "listening" as an example of the Feedback strand.   If we accept Ned Flanders's (1969) two-thirds rule, then two thirds of the time someone is talking in the classroom, and two thirds of that time it is the teacher who is talking.   But, this two-thirds rule is just an average.   In reality, "Flanders found that teachers of high achievers were the talkers about 55 percent of the time.   Teachers of low achievers monopolized 80 percent of the talking, which suggests that the low achievers spend considerably more time listening than being heard" (*TESA*, 1993, p. D-43). The TESA workshop helps to make this fact apparent to participants.

As a third instance, the TESA model defines "higher-level questioning" as part of the Response Opportunities strand. Using Bloom's (1956) *Taxonomy of Educational Objectives, Handbook I: Cognitive Domain,* it is clear that low-achieving students are regularly asked lower level, factual questions, while high-achieving-students are asked higher level, thought-provoking questions. Once again, the TESA workshop participants are made aware of this differential teacher behavior.

An important part of the TESA training involves having participants set SFP-related goals for their classrooms. Several such goals, with reference to the Personal Regard, Feedback, and Response Opportunities instances described above, could be, respectively, "pay the same amount of attention to all students, both high achievers and low achievers," "allow/encourage both high achievers and low achievers to talk," and "challenge both high achievers and low achievers with higher level questions."

TESA participants, working in groups of five (i.e., teachers in the same building or in buildings in close proximity) are released for half a day each month to observe and code fellow teachers' interactions with students. This coded raw data is used by the observed teachers to assess their progress toward equitable positive expectations toward their students.

*TESA Research*

In its over two decades of operation, TESA has had plenty of time and opportunity to be evaluated—often as the subject of doctoral dissertations. Overall, the results are consistent and positive. Most often, TESA-based studies take the form of measuring the overall levels of student achievement (i.e., reading, mathematics) and/or student self-esteem with TESA-trained teachers compared to non-TESA-trained teachers.

In a study by Jones (1990), both student achievement and student self-esteem were measured in classes taught by TESA-trained teachers and non-TESA-trained teachers. Using 37 volunteer, suburban high school reading teachers, Jones found that classes taught by teachers who had been trained through the TESA model did, in fact, have significantly higher reading achievement and self-esteem scores than did classes taught by non-TESA-trained teachers.

In a similarly designed study, but with 20 teachers of mildly handicapped students in Grades 4, 5, and 6, Kohler (1987) found that there was an increase in achievement as measured by the Peabody Individual Achievement Test in the experimental group (TESA-trained teachers) as compared to the control group (non-TESA-trained teachers). No significant differences between experimental and control groups were found in students' self-concept—both groups showed an increase.

Another similar study, this time with 60 at-risk ninth graders, 30 involved in the TESA program (experimental group) and 30 not involved in the TESA program (control group), produced mixed results. Warren (1989) found that although students involved in the experimental group did show significant improvements in scholastic achievement over students in the control group, no significant differences between the two groups were found for changes in total self-esteem and self-concept.

In a longitudinal study with 663 elementary and secondary students, Crumb (1992) measured student achievement before teachers participated in TESA training and again one and two years after teachers had received TESA training. Significant student achievement gains were found for both elementary and secondary school students for TESA-trained teachers. Questionnaires completed by 27 school principals revealed that they judged that the TESA training benefited both high- and low-achieving students and that the program should be continued or expanded.

In a study by Peterson (1989), numerous pretest and posttest measures of teachers' attitudes and students' behaviors and achievement were administered. Although TESA-trained teachers did not produce significant increases in student achievement, a decrease in student absences and discipline referrals did occur in TESA-trained teachers' classrooms.

In a study designed to increase teachers' supportive and motivating interactions with low-achieving students, teachers were trained to increase the use of 10 teacher-student interactions. McConnell (1985) collected data on these teachers prior to and following the training program. The author reported that although significantly more response opportunities were made available to high-achieving students before the training, after the training high-achieving and low-achieving students received equal response opportunities. Further, teachers' proximity and delving (i.e., higher order questioning) behaviors increased significantly for low-achieving students after the teacher training.

Still one more study of TESA, this time by Wetzler (1986), using 24 teachers (12 TESA trained and 12 nontrained) revealed that TESA-trained teachers interacted with their students more often than did teachers who had not received the training. Of special interest is the conclusion that TESA-trained teachers continued to practice the TESA principles two years after the training.

Other similarly constructed studies (i.e., Copper, 1990; Gottfredson, Marciniak, Birdseye, & Gottfredson, 1995; Harris, 1990; Hindalong, 1993; Woehr, 1986), though, have not produced significant differences between TESA-trained teachers (experimental group) and non-TESA-trained teachers (control group). In these studies, any gains noted in student achievement and self-concept for the TESA-trained teachers were not significantly greater than those for the non-TESA-trained teachers.

*A Personal TESA Testimonial*

What follows is a personal testimonial by Paul W. Brenneman, a recently trained TESA instructor. In his testimonial he addresses, (1) why he sought the TESA training, (2) what he thought of the training, and (3) how he has used the training both in his classes and in training other teachers. His personal testimonial on the self-fulfilling prophecy adds credibility to the argument that teachers need to be trained in how to use effectively the self-fulfilling prophecy.

In 1991, I was given the opportunity to attend a workshop designed to train teachers in TESA (teacher expectation, student achievement). As a coordinator, I would then train my fellow faculty members in TESA if my district decided to implement the program. Even after the first day, the program far outdistanced my expectations. Today, I still employ the techniques I learned during my training and, if I may say so, I enjoy a measure of success with them.

Implementing what TESA taught me was immediate and so were the results. Students who I believed could not achieve at a level that was even average began to do above average work. I noticed that my teaching style became more inclusive of all the students in my classroom, not just those who I knew could answer my questions correctly on a regular basis. The opportunity to observe other teachers was invaluable. It was also good to know that if I needed to do some self-evaluation on my effectiveness, I could count on my colleagues to observe one of my lessons.

TESA provided me with the ability to distribute response opportunities equitably, provide individual help, employ latency, delve when appropriate, explore status roles, and employ higher level questioning. It enabled me to better recognize the learning performance of my students through the proper use of feedback. I also learned techniques that made me a better listener. This has helped to show my students that I am concerned for their performance in school as well as about issues that affect their private lives.

In TESA, question and answer wait time is referred to as latency. Teachers, for the most part, do not allow enough time for students to formulate a response after being asked a question. TESA asks teachers to prepare for the implementation of wait time by silently counting to five after asking a question, by telling students that wait time will be extended, and by planning to employ latency in a particular part of a presentation, especially a part emphasizing higher level thinking. The rewards include longer and more in-depth student responses, higher levels of confidence in those responding, fewer failures to respond, and increased participation of slower students.

TESA also taught me about the benefits of delving (eliciting the correct answer from a student through probing and giving clues through suggestive follow-ups). Enhanced student self-esteem as well as improved knowledge are only two important outcomes. Delving has also helped me better evaluate student knowledge, and, in concert with latency, has increased participation in oral. There is no doubt in my mind that the TESA training I received was valuable for me and for my students.

## Other Preservice and/or In-service Training Programs

A study by Weeks (1986) focused upon aspects of interactive teaching strategies rather than upon curriculum offerings. Teachers were trained in the use of specific interactive teaching strategies, such as increased use of praise and allowing more wait-time. By the end of the study, teachers were observed to be using significantly more expectations-related teaching strategies—both with low-achieving and with high-achieving class groups.

Although the TESA program concentrates upon increasing 15 specific teacher-student interaction behaviors, especially with low-achieving students, there are other expectations-type training programs available. One such program, Gender Expectations and Student Achievement (GESA) is a staff development program designed to help teachers identify and remove gender-based classroom biases. GESA, like TESA, uses a combination of workshops, peer coaching, and team approaches to help teachers use more positive interactions (i.e., convey positive expectations) more equitably. According to Lindley and Keithley (1991), GESA programs do develop in teachers a higher level of awareness of issues and a willingness to address these issues in their classrooms.

## CONCLUSION

According to Smith and Luginbuhl (1976), "appropriate training can effectively reduce the potentially negative effects of teacher expectancy on evaluative feedback" (p. 271). Research indicates that knowledge about the SFP combined with actual teaching experiences with student audiences in a variety of ways is most likely to facilitate lasting attitudinal changes in teachers (Evans & Reiff, 1989). Training to raise expectations, in other words, to create a more positive attitude in the minds of both the teachers and the students, is very different from the training that teachers normally receive. Yet, as this chapter has argued, such training is worth the effort.

As important as it is that teachers' attitudes become more positive and subsequent behaviors change (i.e., in quality and frequency of feedback, higher level questioning) toward those for whom they have traditionally held low expectations, this will not be enough. Expectations, high or low, do not operate in a vacuum. In a monograph series by Bamburg (1994) titled *Raising Expectations to Improve Student Learning*, the author states, "If teachers are to change their expectations for students significantly, it is unreasonable to assume that the classroom is the only place where change is needed. Many of the factors contributing to low teacher expectations reside outside of the classroom" (p. 24). Parental involvement, lack of vision by school and community leaders, and lack of resources are among the many other factors that convey expectations to today's youth and, too often, hinder their achievement and motivation. Teachers alone cannot be expected to bring the self-fulfilling prophecy in check; but they surely can help.

Although TESA training attemps to impact teachers' expectations of students, it may be possible to target students, themselves, for training in raising their teachers' expectations of them. This approach of training subordinates to change the expectations superiors hold of them has worked in industry (Shimko, 1989, 1990). Perhaps it could work in education, too.

## ENDNOTE

1. The address for the Los Angeles County Office of Education is 9300 E. Imperial Highway, Downey, CA 90242.

# PART III

# SFP APPLICATIONS

Chapter 15 in part 3 presents a collection of twelve 1,000-word self-fulfilling prophecy personal testimonials written from the viewpoint of theorists and practitioners, with an emphasis upon the latter. Chapter 16 introduces the reader to ERIC (Educational Resources Information Center) a readily available information and dissemination system that educators can use to learn still more about the theory and practice surrounding the self-fulfilling prophecy.

# CHAPTER 15

# PRACTITIONER TESTIMONIALS

Testimonial writers have been solicited based upon their unique educational positions. Their testimonials address both the problems associated with the abuse of the SFP and the benefits of its positive use.

## EXPECTATIONS: ELEMENTARY TO ELEMENTARY SUCCESS

### Contributor: James J. Tracy, Elementary School Principal

James Jay Tracy, principal of Klein Elementary School, Harbor Creek School, in Erie, PA, is in the final stages of completing his D.Ed. in School Administration from the State University of New York at Buffalo. He is certified as an elementary and secondary school principal, a high school biology and general science teacher, and a school superintendent. He has taught for 8 years, been a middle school principal for 3 years, and served as an elementary school principal for 10 years. He is currently the principal at Klein School, a suburban elementary school. Professionally, Mr. Tracy has contributed as a practitioner reactant to the *Journal of Classroom Management* and as one of the contributing authors for the book *Classroom Management: Theory and Practice* (1995).

### Testimonial

As an elementary school principal, I cannot emphasize enough the importance of expectations in the education and the development of young children. Elementary-age children tend to live up to what their teachers expect of them.

Helping the children to believe in themselves is as important as teaching the curriculum content. High expectations and appropriate positive verbal praise help the students to believe that they can achieve. Unfortunately, continual negative comments and negative one-line zingers cause the children to live up to expectations of poor academic performance and/or poor behavior as well.

I have seen students struggle through a school year with little success and then turn around the following year and do quite well. The difference, I believe, is what the teachers expected of their students. When a child perceives that the teacher expects poor achievement, the child begins to believe that he or she cannot do the work and lives up to the expectations of poor performance. The successful teacher is able to communicate to the child that he or she can do the tasks assigned, provides for situations of success for the child to experience, and gives positive verbal praise to encourage the student. This causes the child to believe that he or she can do the assigned tasks, and the student lives up to these expectations of successful academic performance.

Our recently "included" special education students do much better work at a more difficult level now that they are in the regular education setting all day. The students have indicated that they do not feel as different as they did when they had to go to a special room. This belief, coupled with good teaching strategies, has caused the children to live up to their expectations of success in the regular classroom setting. Furthermore, the students have indicated that when they were being "pulled out," they believed that it was because they could not do the regular work.

A student who came to our school from another district was labeled as a discipline problem. His records were filled with discipline letters. The child's parent felt that her child's behavior deteriorated because he was living up to what the teacher expected of him. Right or wrong, I kept this young man's records from the teacher for his first 6 weeks in our district. He was assigned to a teacher with outstanding classroom organization and control. The teacher clearly related her academic and behavioral expectations for the boy. The boy apparently believed he was to behave in a certain manner, and he fulfilled these expectations. The teacher was surprised to find out that the child had a severe discipline problem in his prior school, and she disregarded the reports in the boy's file.

For the past several years, I have not recorded ability index scores directly on the students' records. I had found that teachers were telling parents things like, "A 'C' grade is good for your child because his or her ability is in the low end of average." If a teacher is saying this, then she or he is probably only expecting C work from the child. When the youngster perceives this, that child will live up to the expectations of a C student.

I recall one student who was doing extremely well until the teacher saw the child's very low ability score toward the end of the year. The teacher began to doubt if the child could do the work. The child perceived this and began to struggle. The following year, the teacher did not see the student's ability score and expected the girl to do well. She completed the year with all A grades.

Certainly ability plays a role in what a child can do, but I have seen children with high expectations and low ability do extremely well. Unfortunately, I have seen children with high ability and low expectations perform very poorly. This is why it is essential that both teachers and parents help children to develop high expectations of themselves and that they then provide the situations for success to occur.

Educators many times do not realize the power of expectations. I have seen beginning readers struggle because they believed they could not read well. Each time they began to read they would start with, "I can't do this very well." Teachers have to help the child change his or her expectation of being a poor reader to that of being a good reader. It seems that when the teacher expects the child to be a good reader and provides positive experiences and good instruction, students believe they can read well—and they do.

It is essential that teachers and parents convey high expectations to their children through their words and actions. When a child believes these positive expectations, he or she will generally live up to them and do well. The positive use of expectations can be a powerful tool for a teacher.

## PREPARING WHITE TEACHERS TO TEACH IN CLASSROOMS OF COLOR—EXPECTATIONS COUNT!

### Contributor: Shirley J. Bowles, Associate Professor

Shirley J. Bowle, Ed.D., is an associate professor with the Department of Educational Leadership and Research and Curriculum and Instruction, respectively, in the College of Education and Psychology at the University of Southern Mississippi. Before coming to the university, she worked for over 20 years in the public schools of Mississippi as a teacher, counselor, and parent coordinator. Since coming to USM, where she teachers courses in curriculum development, multicultural education, secondary education methods, and foundations of education, she has published several articles related to her research interests in multiculturalism and cultural diversity in the classroom.

### Testimonial

I found it extremely difficult to determine what format this testimonial should take. A large part of my effort in developing it came from speaking with students, faculty, staff, and administrators, many of whom are on traditional black campuses. In writing this testimonial, I also reviewed my own perceptions and experiences, including discussions with others during the four years I have been a black faculty member on a predominantly white campus. The consistency with which these various sources reinforced the same information—the frustration, the pain, and most assuredly the existence of being on the inside (but still on the outside)—was almost eerie.

The experiences and qualifications that made me feel I did have something to contribute included my work in conducting staff development workshops on cultural awareness for school districts in Mississippi and the presentations I had made at major conferences throughout the United States. Therefore, I can address the topic of the self-fulfilling prophecy (SFP) as an observer, a collector of evidence, a witness of the SFP, and most certainly as a victim. My goal is to synthesize my own impressions and experiences as well as those of the other sources I discuss.

The concept of SFP has already been defined, but I will speak briefly to the definition of SFP. The concept of SFP conjures up the idea of teacher labeling, and the process of students responding to what the labels imply. This labeling process can be found in every nook and cranny of society. My colleagues in the Department of Education and Psychology gave me their definition of SFP—expectations bring about performance. Therefore, given these definitions, SFP as it relates to education is a dramatic illustration of how teachers' (or one person's) behavior can trigger students' (another person's) expectations. I have witnessed and experienced SFP in school settings, and not only have I come to recognize the negative attitudes of others, but I have come to recognize some of my own attitudes and behaviors as they relate to teacher expectations. For instance, I found myself academically stereotyping a black male student. When I became aware of my behavior, I changed the environment and gave that student the power and insight that allowed him to intervene and say, "No, that's not me. That is a label you have created about me." Consequently, his academic behavior changed. The change was triggered by my response to him.

During my second year as a faculty member in higher education, I conducted a survey entitled "Attitudes and Perceptions of Student Teachers Toward Diversity." When reviewing the results, I was mortified to read that the majority of these aspirant teachers believed that students are responsible for their own failure in school. It was clear that the teachers were more willing to blame students for their (teachers') own failures. If this differential expectation is communicated to the students in one way or another, the expectation will create or perpetuate the failure. Attitudes and perceptions are germane to the theme of SFP (Crescimanno, 1982). Perception precedes experience. If one is not made aware, then, these preconceptions will govern the process of perception.

Now I would like to turn to some demographics gathered in Mississippi. In my search for information while putting together this testimonial, nothing was more striking to me than student enrollment and retention figures in this state. These findings are truly remarkable. They revealed that 35.6% of the population is black, the largest fraction of any state in the nation. If current trends continue, population projections suggest that the proportion of blacks in Mississippi will rise to about 40% by the year 2000.

Approximately 50% of white students graduated within 5 years of beginning their baccalaureate degree, 30% of students who were neither white nor black graduated within 5 years, and 25% of black students graduated within 5 years. These statistics do not tell us why the completion rate of black students is less than half that of white students or why other students of color are far less likely than white students to graduate within 5 years. We can only speculate. Some will say that students of color do not perform as well as white students. If this is part of the answer, then we have to ask Why. Does teacher expectation influence black students' performance? It certainly seems likely. Banks and Banks (1993) report that when teacher expectations are reflected in their behavior toward children, these expectations are related to students' cognitive changes, even when pupil IQ and achievement are controlled. However, negative expectations appear to have more powerful consequences than do positive expectations. We need to know whether the retention problems of students of color in Mississippi are a result of negative teacher expectation or some other factors. I suggest to you that the SFP is not positive as it relates to teacher expectations of people of color, whether these people are faculty, students, or staff.

I do not think that I am unique in having observed the negative dynamics of the SFP. For example, I have observed teachers allowing those students for whom they have high expectations more time to answer questions, praising them more often, and generally being less critical of them. I have also watched this expectation spread into peer associations. Generally, those students who are looked upon favorably by teachers are also regarded favorably by students. The issue of invisibility is an issue that is relevant to the self-fulfilling prophecy. Many students of color report having similar research papers or essays to ones of their peers who received higher grades. There is also the expectation of some faculty members that black students do not know how to write. Accordingly, when we speculate on why the percentage of black students has consistently decreased in the past 10 years and why the retention rates of black students fall so far behind those of white students, it seems logical to conclude that a large factor is teacher expectation.

It is recognized that students are not the only victims of negative SFP. How, then, do the findings on students' experiences of negative teacher expectation relate and compare to faculty of color's experiences of the self-fulfilling prophecy? My perceptions, experiences of witnessing the SFP with faculty, and discussions I have had with other faculty convince me that most of the same dynamics are behind the SFP that the students experience.

I argue that five things contribute a great deal to the SFP so often at work in schools: (1) the labeling process operating in schools, (2) the expectations of teachers, (3) the curriculum and teaching styles, (4) the sorting and selection process, and (5) the social characteristics of students.

It is clear that much work needs to be done to further our understanding of the SFP. One implication that emerges from this testimonial is that the SFP is virtually always destructive, but it need not be construed so negatively. On the contrary, the effects of the SFP can produce conditions that foster positive interpersonal perceptions. However, as this process becomes more fully understood, we expect to see the development of improved teacher-student relationships and resulting student success.

## A SECONDARY SCHOOL PRINCIPAL'S VIEW OF THE IMPORTANCE OF EXPECTATIONS

### Contributor: David Tompkins, Principal (Retired)

Dr. Tompkins's career in education spans thirty-five years, including coaching, teaching science (7-12), and seventeen years of high school administration at Iroquois High School, Erie, PA. Although now retired from basic education, he continues to teach on an adjunct basis at Gannon University in both the undergraduate and graduate programs of teacher education. From an international perspective, Dr. Tompkins has had the opportunity to be part of a study team that made numerous observations in the schools of New South Wales, Australia. He holds four degrees, two from Edinboro University of Pennsylvania and two from Michigan State University.

### Testimonial

One of the most difficult problems for teachers is to find ways to motivate their students. Many of the useful factors and techniques seem to be closely intertwined with an individual's personality. Traits such as a colorful personality, showmanship, warmth, and empathy seem to be inherent or perhaps shaped over such a long period of time that I as a high school principal have had limited success in suggesting that a person make significant changes in these aspects. Yet a principal cannot escape the obligation to help new teachers develop the traits and behaviors that will enable them to relate successfully to their students.

If you analyze those teachers who have had an unusual degree of success in motivating students, I suspect that several factors will emerge. There's a story that I like to tell new teachers that represents one of these factors. We had been in a period of decline in our football program to the extent that we had experienced three losing seasons in succession. A coaching change was made, and there was a dramatic turnabout in the team's performance. One of our social studies teachers asked a senior player who was seeing limited playing time why the team was having success when for the most part the team was composed of the same players as last year. His response was, "The coach believes in us. He expects us to win." Further discussion revealed that the previous coach apparently let the team know prior to facing each opponent that the odds were against their winning.

Clearly, one of the factors in this situation was positive expectation. The new coach was benefiting from communicating high expectations. Because of his expectations, the players set a different level of expectation for themselves, which translated into an improved performance on the playing field. Imagine that. Player motivation could be changed just by creating a picture of success in the mind's eye of those young men. You might wonder why that player's comments stick with me to this day. It has a lot to do with who that young athlete was. You see, he was not a star, nor even a first team player, but rather a young person who because of a birth defect had a serious leg deformity. That same coach would put him in as a defensive lineman to spell another player. Bruce knew that the coach expected him to do the job of the more agile first stringers. It was amazing what the coach's belief in Bruce did for the other players. Once convinced of the power of expectations, I have tried to influence staff to look at positive expectation as a seed of optimism that germinates success.

But you don't need to stay with athletics to find examples of how expectations can influence young people. In a nearby middle school, there is a teacher of a life skills class who uses optimism and positive expectations to change behavior. Many of her students are Down's syndrome youngsters, and some are autistic. Often they were the brunt of teasing and name-calling by some of the bullies and rowdy elements of the school. Mrs. Carrie surprised the guidance counselor by asking if two of the worst offenders could be scheduled into her class for one entire morning session. After clearing it with the building principal, the two boys were brought down to her class.

The teacher began by introducing the boys to her class as through they were very special guests. Whenever she could, she included them in the first lessons for the morning. When the boys participated in positive ways, she would ask her class to celebrate their success. Many of her students by their very nature are warm and demonstrative. They were accustomed to supporting each other's behavior with praise and applause. Even a casual observer could see that the boys were basking in a hero's light. The impact of changing the expectations for the boys was dramatic.

Consider the reaction of the teachers who did not have to teach the bullies that morning. Later at lunch they queried Mrs. Carrie with questions such as: "Did you have to send them to the office?" "Why would you ever take those two boys together if you did not have to? I can't handle them one at a time when they are in my classroom." Too often I have seen negative expectations such as these set the pattern for continuing problems. For some reason teachers are more likely to share horror stories with embellishments. Perhaps it's an impact of the societal way that the media saturates us with bad news, but whatever the cause, the result is that those staff yet to deal with the "bad news kids" begin to establish a negative frame of expectation before they deal with the student.

Well, what was the outcome of the bullies' class visit with Mrs. Carrie? Today they are the hallway guardians of her special needs kids. Nobody seems to want to tease her students because they have seen the hand-slapping "high fives" as Mrs. Carrie's kids pass their former tormentors. What a great example of taking a positive approach to a problem.

As the result of my experiences, I encourage new staff members to spend little if any time in the faculty room. It's too easy to pick up negative expectations for the students they have yet to face. Whenever possible I try to link new staff to veteran staff to serve as their mentors. One of the prime requisites of mentors is that they hold positive expectations for students. Not only do good teachers have to believe that learning is possible, they have to translate that belief to students. I believe that those teachers who operate from a positive frame of reference have the best chance of making a difference in the lives of their students.

## SELF-FULFILLING PROPHECY: THE COMMUNICATION CONNECTION

### Contributor: Cathy Sargent Mester, Senior Lecturer

Cathy Sargent Mester is Senior Lecturer in Speech Communication at The Pennsylvania State University, The Behrend College, Erie, PA, where she has been a faculty member since 1971. In addition to that professional teaching experience, she has done numerous years of volunteer teaching at the elementary and secondary levels. She has researched and published journal articles and books in the areas of religious communication and communication in education, and she has been an active workshop leader for educators as well as professionals in business and industry. She is well positioned to discuss how expectations can be conveyed appropriately and inappropriately through the medium of speech.

### Testimonial

Fundamentally, human communication is a process grounded in the exchange of symbols. Symbols typically used are, of course, words and nonverbal expressions. The real importance of the symbolic nature of human communication is that those symbols only represent the user's perception of reality—the symbol is not the reality. Consequently, when a 5 foot, 3 inch woman is described as short, that does not mean that she is, by any objective definition, short. It simply means that whoever is doing the describing finds her to be short compared to others in his or her frame of reference.

So, there is a difference, then, between what is real and the words we exchange about the reality as we personally perceive it. This is an important principle, as it relates to the self-fulfilling prophecy. It means that the way we speak of our expectations of one another or of ourselves does not necessarily convey *reality-based* expectations, but rather *perception-based* expectations. Further, the way we interpret others' words about their expectations of us will be a perception-based interpretation, not a reality-based interpretation.

Let's take another look at the earlier example of the woman described as short. Thinking of herself as short probably would not significantly affect her achievement of most of her life's goals. She may avoid reaching for items on high shelves because she assumes them to be outside her reach; but that is no great loss. On the other hand, if that person labeled "short" were an aspiring athlete, avoiding opportunities to reach beyond his or her perceived grasp would affect the achievement of life goals.  What if Muggsy Bogues (5-foot, 3-inch starting point guard for the NBA's Charlotte Hornets) had interpreted his shortness as a reality-based description?  What would he have avoided doing because he believed the label to be accurate and unarguable?  His acceptance of that description of himself might have limited his willingness to work at being a good basketball player.  Thus, he would have been victimized by the self-fulfilling prophecy.

We signal our expectations of others both with our words and with our nonverbal messages.  The verbal and nonverbal labels we choose may convey either positive or negative expectations.  Either way, they ultimately may become self-fulfilling prophecies.  As communicators trying to make appropriate rhetorical choices, we must keep that impact in mind.

Concretely, these principles ought to lead us to make verbal and nonverbal choices geared to setting up positive expectations in our listeners.  For instance, when leading any kind of a meeting and asking for volunteers, choose words that communicate an expectation that people will want to volunteer.  Phrasing such as, "We can only take the first five volunteers," conveys a much more flattering expectation than the pleading, "Plea-ea-ease won't somebody volunteer for this project?"  Likewise, the teacher who wants the students to study diligently for an important test should describe the test as "challenging" instead of saying, "I don't think it's too hard" or "This will be a very hard test."  In the second case, the students will not think they need to study, and in the third they will think that there is no point in their studying because they will not do well anyway.  The resultant grades will likely reflect those expectations.  Their actions, triggered by your words, were a self-fulfilling prophecy.

Nonverbal behaviors similarly set up prophetic expectations.  The teacher who asks a question of the class while having his/her arms akimbo or crossed subtly conveys a negative expectation of the quality of the class response.  That behavior is a self-fulfilling prophecy in that it increases the likelihood that the students will feel too intimidated to provide good answers to the question.

There has been considerable research on the question of gender bias on the part of teachers.  It seems that many teachers subconsciously have higher expectations of male students than of female students.  By inadvertently conveying those expectations via the nonverbal tools of eye contact and posturing, they encourage more males to be attentive and participatory than females, thus fulfilling their unspoken prophecy.

So, as teachers, we should be sensitive to how our words, our facial expressions, and our posture, for example, convey expectations to our students that will affect their performance.  We should choose verbal and nonverbal symbols that encourage positive, constructive, and appropriate behaviors from all the students.

In so doing, not only do we impact student response, we also impact our own attitudes and behaviors.  By giving voice to our thoughts, beliefs, and feelings, we make them more real and more credible. So, by saying out loud (or adopting a related nonverbal expression) that Johnny or Susie can do good work, we talk ourselves into that belief as real. The same prophetic effect can be felt with negative statements as well. Saying out loud at the start of the day, for instance, "Today is going to be a lonnnng day," makes the day seem to drag. A recent news item makes the point strikingly. In reporting a very serious accident with her horse, a woman said she kept saying to the horse, "You're going to be fine." As she noted, she needed to say that not so much for the horse as for herself—she needed to believe it, and saying the words made them credible and, hence, therapeutic. The same holds true for the teacher who chooses to say, "This will be an exciting class."

In communication classes, we always talk about making careful rhetorical choices, for what separates the successful communicator from the unsuccessful is the quality of the choices made about what to say and how to say it. The choices that are best are those that are appropriate to the particular rhetorical situation—the nature of the listeners and the setting in which the communication takes place.

When the communication setting is a classroom and the audience is students, the same principles apply. We contribute to everyone's perception of that dynamic reality by the words and nonverbal expressions we choose to use. Part of that is the way we as teachers convey both appropriately and inappropriately our expectations of ourselves and of the class through the medium of speech.

## IMPACT OF THE SELF-FULFILLING PROPHECY ON SPECIAL EDUCATION

### Contributor: Debra K. Stein, Assistant Professor

Debra K. Stein received her M.A. and Ph.D. in developmental psychology from Temple University. She has worked in the area of education for sixteen years. She has taught at The Pennsylvania State University and Rowan College of New Jersey, her current affiliation. Dr. Stein has supervised educational programs for developmentally disabled and learning disabled children and youth and has consulted with school districts in Pennsylvania and New Jersey on curriculum development and program planning. She has spoken at professional conferences and workshops across the United States.

### Testimonial

Since the 1960s, psychologists have been investigating the teacher-expectancy effect otherwise known as the Pygmalion effect of self-fulfilling prophecy. However, teachers and students have understood the workings of the phenomenon for centuries, and anecdotal reports abound describing the impact that preset expectations have on a student's successes and failures.

I believe that the self-fulfilling prophecy has been the most damaging in the realm of special education—a discipline which is chock-full of labels. These labels are assigned altruistically in an attempt to secure special instruction and services for students with exceptional problems or talents. However, when these labels are evaluated pragmatically, they are seen to result in singling out some children as "problem children," thus clearly alerting the teacher to expect an abnormal performance profile. My experiences as a developmental psychologist, a supervisor of special education, as a school consultant, and as a parent of a gifted–learning disabled child have all repeatedly put me into situations in which I have witnessed the self-fulfilling prophecy at work.

While operating as a supervisor of special education at a private school for the developmentally disabled, it was my responsibility to meet annually with the special education directors of school districts served by the private school to discuss the progress of the students placed in our care. I cannot forget the circumstances surrounding the educational placement of a multiply disabled child who had severe cerebral palsy. The cerebral palsy affected her motor skills, but as far as we could determine, not her intellectual potential. The child in question was confined to a wheelchair and had no ability to control her arms or legs or to speak. She had been attending this private school since infancy, and upon reaching the age of 7 had actually advanced beyond the elementary school curriculum that the school was able to offer. This situation occurred because her peers at the school were almost all diagnosed mentally retarded and, of course, she was not. Fortunately, a teacher who had worked with the child for 2 years was able to determine the knowledge level of the child through watching the child's eye movements and gross changes in body position (the child would stiffen her body when she became excited). The teacher even taught the child to read and thus was convinced that this child was not mentally retarded and that she needed to continue her education with nonretarded peers in a public school setting. She spoke with the parents and me, and procedures were initiated to have the child transferred to public school.

For 3 years we met with officials from the child's school district and tried to get them to consider placing the child in public school. Again and again, we were told that she did not belong because of the seriousness of her physical handicaps and the questionableness of her level of intelligence. As the expectancy effect would predict, the officials actually thought the child was mentally disabled because she attended a school for the mentally disabled. They reviewed her records and made in-class observations, yet they just could not "see" her intellectual potential. Even the child's parents, who desperately wanted her to be in school with her peers, came to question whether or not she would be able to make it in public school and started to focus on their daughter's deficits rather than her gifts. However, the strength of the teacher's expectancies and beliefs did not waiver, and at the subsequent year's meeting, when the child was almost 10 years old, the school district finally agreed to accept her enrollment into a public school classroom. To this day, 5 years later, she remains with her peers and is doing fine.

Unfortunately, reports relating consequences of the self-fulfilling prophecy do not always have such a happy outcome. It is a commonly known fact that many gifted and talented students do not perform to their potential on a daily basis and many even fail because the people who interact with them ignore their giftedness or criticize them for it. Not expecting gifted children to perform contributes to mediocrity and underachievement. Creating an atmosphere of dislike or disturbance at having to deal with a "gifted individual" contributes to obstinacy and behavior problems. I have heard it said that the intellectual potential of the gifted and talented in our culture is becoming our most wasted natural resource. This may be true, given that many school districts are forced to move away from arranging special educational opportunities for the cognitively gifted because of budgetary constraints. These students must fend for themselves in the regular classroom. Such a noninterventionist approach is rationalized by the belief that "if these kids are so gifted, then they can restructure the curriculum on their own and get the most out of it."

Perhaps the most telling of the circumstances involving gifted children arises when we have a child dually diagnosed as both learning disabled and gifted. Which should you expect—that her performance should show difficulties or that her performance should be exceptional? More often than not, teachers expect and focus on the difficulties, making these primary in the child's eyes, thus diminishing self-esteem, rather then focusing on the gifts and enhancing self-esteem. An excellent illustration of this is what happened when our family moved to a new school district and I attempted to get my gifted–learning disabled daughter placed in a gifted education program. The school district used reading to place their students in the program, and my daughter's disability is language related. (Her reading scores are about average but not exceptional.) Although her IQ test scores qualified her for the special program, the school district resisted. Although agreeing in the end to place her in the special program, the teacher (a reading specialist who had previously spoken with the school principal) expected my daughter to have difficulty with the class, and so her performance constantly fluctuated between unsatisfactory and satisfactory, with rarely an outstanding grade appearing on her report. After withdrawing her from the program (and the school) and placing her in a different educational environment that valued her talent in math, she was placed in an accelerated math program where she is expected to perform on a par with the rest of the class. To this day, three years later, she consistently scores above the 95th percentile on all standardized mathematics tests.

These cases have been chosen to show how the expectations of those with whom we come in contact affect our expectations of ourselves—and thus our performance. As social beings we are constantly at risk and are even trained on a nonconscious level to do what others want. When a label is placed defining explicit expectations in behavior, we find ourselves even more potently influenced. Let's read and reread this textbook so that we may become more aware of how our behavior affects others and ultimately become more aware of how these expectations affect our evaluation of ourselves.

## A VOCATIONAL-TECHNICAL SCHOOL COUNSELOR'S VIEW OF THE SFP

### Contributor: Patty Palo, Counselor

Patty Palo has worked for 8 years at the Erie County Technical School (ECTS), one of approximately 80 area vocational technical schools in Pennsylvania. She has served in the capacity of guidance counselor, admissions representative, and acting principal. Prior to her employment with the ECTS, Mrs. Palo worked at Hermit Medical Center as an education consultant on the Inpatient Child Psychiatric Ward, as well as in Human Resources as an educational specialist. She is married to a fellow educator, Deny Palo, and they are the proud parents of two sons. The Palo family tries to live the self-fulfilled prophecy through mutual encouragement and love in their home and work.

### Testimonial

In considering the notion of the self-fulfilling prophecy, I must smile and ask the question, Self-fulfilling prophecy—who would doubt or question it once you have experienced our school, the Erie County Area Vocational Technical School? I take this stance because of my personal and professional experiences with the concept of SFP. Personally, I come from a background that encouraged, enforced, and believed in the philosophy that one should set one's expectations and beliefs high and they will be attained. Professionally, the ECTS staff strives to implement this on a daily basis. Not only believe it, but live it.

The implementation and reality of the SFP come to mind in two specific areas at ECTS. I see the beliefs of the staff and the roles we play in the lives of our students and, for that matter, the survival and image of our school as essential attestations of the SFP. Let me explain each. Students come to our school from 10 Erie County schools located around the city of Erie, Pennsylvania. Eight years ago, when I started at the ECTS, the enrollment was approximately 500 students; currently we have over 770. The need for us to increase enrollment was paramount. Jobs were in jeopardy, and a couple of programs were part-time. The SFP was evident because the belief of the staff at that time was, Yes, we can and we will improve enrollment. Because this philosophy was integral among all staff members, we assumed that enrollment growth would happen. Indeed it did. When we had the focus of success in mind, all endeavors led to the attainment of it. I am certain that we did not consciously pump ourselves up with the idea of growth, yet it became a part of our life. We lived it. The concepts of Johari's Window and Gordon's Ladder are integrated into this belief. We were functioning at the consciously unskilled level and needed to become consciously skilled and eventually to operate at the unconsciously skilled level. When functioning at the unconsciously skilled level, we find that we act without thinking and that we are effective without having to work at it. We are among the few vocational-technical schools in Pennsylvania who are enjoying an increased population of students. We increased the population because we believed we could!

It is the desire of the ECTS to provide an environment in which each student can and will succeed. Opportunities are provided through which the students can explore visually, auditorially, and/or kinesthetically-tactually. Vocational educators have the opportunity to provide many learning experiences for students in the various learning modalities. We attempt to become consciously skilled, and before we know it, we are functioning at the unconsciously skilled level. It is when the belief of the SFP is totally integrated into the beings of the staff and students that one is a believer and a doer. In keeping with the philosophy that all can and will succeed, the expectation of success is set. We intend that each and every student will meet with success and that every student who walks through the doors will also believe in himself or herself. The ECTS philosophy is that if you attend ECTS, you will be treated as an adult, will act like an adult, and you will be prepared to function in the everyday world as an adult. This philosophy is shared with prospective students during the orientation process, and each student experiences it when he or she participates in the on-site visit.

The proof is in the pudding. We have the pleasant opportunity to see alumni often. Daily, our co-op and high school offices have graduates returning to visit their instructors and talk with them. They come in on their days off from work or college. When asked about their experiences at the ECTS, one hears the consistent message, "My instructor knew me. He believed in me." "I was treated like a person, an adult. I was trusted and encouraged." In essence, the SFP rules at ECTS, and we are proud of it!

## GENDER EQUITY AND THE SELF-FULFILLING PROPHECY

### Contributor: Lynn H. Fox, Psychologist and Assistant Professor

Lynn H. Fox is a psychologist and assistant professor of education at the American University in Washington, D.C. Her research has focused upon the gifted child, particularly mathematically gifted girls, and the importance of teacher training in technology. She is the author of a monograph, *Women and the Problem of Mathematics*, and coeditor of three books: *Mathematical Talent: Discovery, Description, and Development*; *Women and the Mathematical Mystique*; and *The Learning Disabled and Gifted Child*.

### Testimonial

Recently I observed an accelerated seventh-grade mathematics class. You could have drawn a line down the middle to separate the male and female students. The teacher didn't assign the seats this way. "It just happened," she said. The teacher didn't think it was a problem, even though her overhead projector was clearly positioned in the center of the columns of seats in which males sat. The girls had to crane their necks to see the overheads. Informal discussions with some of the girls indicated that they did not like their algebra class, but they couldn't explain why. They probably knew at a subconscious level that they were invisible to the teacher, although they did not directly refer to the fact that the class was segregated by gender or that the teacher seemed to look and talk only to the boys. They could only say that algebra was "boring" or that they didn't see "why anyone would need to know it."

In their book *Failing at Fairness: How America's Schools Cheat Girls* (1994), Myra and David Sadker describe their nearly two decades of observations in classrooms all over the United States and at every grade level, including college. They expose the micro-inequities that occur daily and link this imbalance in attention to the girls' loss of achievement and self-esteem. Consider the following conclusions from their work:

- At every level of schooling, girls receive less teacher attention and less useful teacher feedback. The gap is greatest at the college level.
- Girls talk significantly less than boys do in class. They are eight times less likely than boys to call out comments.
- The contributions of women in history and science are lacking in most curricula; most textbooks depict a male-dominated world.

Recent research points to the relationship between academic achievement and self-esteem. Students who do well in school feel better about themselves, and, in turn, they then feel more capable. For most females, this connection has a negative twist, and a cycle of loss is put into motion. As girls feel less good about themselves, their academic performance declines, and this poor performance further erodes their confidence. This pattern is particularly powerful in math and science classes, with only 18% of middle school girls describing themselves as good in these subjects, down from 31% in elementary school. It is not surprising that the testing gap between boys and girls is particularly wide in mathematics and science, where teachers may be the most blatant in conveying negative expectations for girls.

When we talk with our preservice education students at the American University about these issues, the female students often explode with their own stories of being ignored or even "put down" by a teacher in front of a class. Many males are at first shocked by the stories. When these males begin to observe patterns of teacher-student interactions more closely, especially in college mathematics and science classes, they must concede that the women's stories are real.

Fortunately, we can show our prospective teachers that there are many things they can do to promote equity.  For example, they can easily change seating arrangements in their classes to encourage more interactions with girls and can be encouraged to share their reasons for this with the students.  This may help make students aware of the problem and encourage them to become part of the solution.  When self-selection operates to the disadvantage of one group in terms of long-term consequences, teachers can respond by eliminating choice (an example might be the use of microcomputers in the classroom at the elementary school level).  Another technique involves wait time, the time that teachers allow to elapse between asking a question and eliciting a response from students.  Increasing the duration of wait time from less than a second to 3 to 5 seconds seems to lead to several desirable outcomes.  Teachers increase the number of higher order questions, decrease the number of low-level questions for everyone, and participation rates for girls improve.

Teachers can observe or videotape one another and analyze their behaviors.  Some teachers find that they need to rely on a system to help them break the habit of calling on the same boys too much.  They can put student names on a deck of file cards, shuffle them in each class, and call on the children in random order.  At the elementary level, assigning tasks along the lines of gender stereotypes can be reduced by using alphabetical lists and systematically rotating names for chores like line leader or workbook collector.

At the secondary level it may be important to look at differences in enrollment patterns.  Counselors and teachers can be encouraged to actively recruit young women for advanced courses such as AP calculus or physics.  Sometimes more dramatic interventions are necessary.  One large suburban school system in the mid-Atlantic region had no girls enrolled in their technology classes in high school.  To correct this, they converted the required general ninth grade science class to a 2-hour period of integrated science and technology.  Clearly this type of administrative support for change is more potent than just encouraging girls to take optional courses or encouraging counselors and teachers to be more proactive in recruiting students for sex-segregated classes.  In many school systems, this type of intervention has occurred in the areas of home economics and technology by creating a rotating wheel of electives so that all students get some exposure, usually in the middle school grades, to both the home economics course and the technology course which is replacing what used to be called "shop."

At all grade levels, teachers should look at the curriculum, especially the text materials.  Where are the women?  How visible are women as role models in the readings and class discussions?  Teachers should be encouraged to develop a repertoire of ideas to incorporate more emphasis on women's contributions in their choices of topics for reports and source materials.

More than half of the population of the world is female.  We must nurture the intellect and talents of women.  Teacher education programs must help to make teachers and future teachers aware of the subtle but still stifling effect of communicating lower career and achievement expectations for girls.  Girls can only achieve parity with boys when teachers have created a gender-fair classroom environment.

## HISPANICS' SCHOOL FAILURE: WHICH CAME FIRST, THE EXPECTATIONS OR THE REALITY?

### Contributor: Dolores Bonctati, Clinical Therapist

Born of farm-working Mexican-American parents in the San Joaquin Valley of Central California, Dolores Bonetati soon realized that hard work and an education was her way to a better future. She earned a B.A. degree from California State University in Fullerton, and then completed the Teacher Credential Program at the same university. She received her master's degree in Marriage, Family, and Child Counseling from the University of California in Los Angeles. Ms. Bonetati then embarked on a long and productive career with an emphasis on serving those on the lower end of the socioeconomic scale. Using her bilingual skills, she taught elementary school, worked in social services, and is currently employed in mental health services as a clinical psychologist for San Bernardino County.

### Testimonial

When we want to gain new insight, it must be our first concern to make us free from old prejudiced opinion.

—Bacon, 1621

According to the principle of the self-fulfilling prophecy, students live up, or down, to the expectations that others have for them. Researchers using a variety of methods have confirmed the basic principle that teachers' expectations "can and do function as self-fulfilling prophecies" (Brophy & Good, 1974, p. 32). This principle has important implications for minority groups and poor children. Since many middle-class teachers may be convinced (often subconsciously) that such students have intellectual limitations, they convey their expectations to the children, thus getting from them the little that they expect. Most of the research in this area has focused on the majority population. Thus, research on minority populations is scarce, especially relative to Hispanics.

In the United States education system, the Hispanic has historically been associated with the low-achieving status of the lower class minorities. Yet they are one of the fastest growing, largest, and youngest minority groups in the United States. However, compared to the majority population, Hispanics are still disadvantaged in terms of educational and occupational attainment. Research indicates that 40% to 50% of Hispanic students drop out of school before they complete high school. This is more than double the rate for blacks, and three times higher than that for white students. Exactly how many of these students are recent immigrants and how many are native-born U.S. citizens is unknown, but we do know that a large population remains undereducated and undervalued.

Perhaps it is time to focus more on what teachers specifically say and do to convey their negative expectations. In a doctoral dissertation, one researcher reported that he found much discrimination against Hispanics in the community and school system. The teachers were all Caucasians and seemed unanimous in sharing the stereotype of Hispanics as being inferior in capacity as well as performance. Sociometric tests indicated that even the Hispanic children came to share the view that had been constantly held up to them that Caucasians are smarter than Hispanics. The Caucasian teachers in the study characterized Hispanics as being immoral, violent, belligerent, dirty, unintelligent, irresponsible, and lazy.

It is my belief that teachers, in general, are not sensitive to the sociocultural differences between Hispanic and Caucasian children. While teachers are aware of some obvious differences in language, customs, and experience backgrounds, they are not aware of underlying value conflicts. For example, one study by Delgado-Gaitan and Trueba (1985) accurately interprets Hispanic children's copying in the classroom as a legitimate activity since it is based upon home socialization patterns that stress collectively and social cohesiveness. Caucasian teachers often misinterpret the copying by Hispanics as a practice characterizing dishonest, lazy, and poorly motivated students and indicating low academic ability. It is clear that teachers' expectations may be influenced by the failure to understand value conflicts.

Different types of teachers express high or low expectations in different ways. Some teachers believe that they can and will influence student learning. However, some teachers believe that student intelligence levels are fixed. Findings also suggest that teachers form quick judgments about their students and that they develop clear expectations for the performance of their students early in the year. This is demonstrated by comments made during interviews on the third day of school by a group of first-grade teachers. The children had not been to kindergarten, had not taken tests, and had not had prior contact with the teachers. Students' sex, social class, and physical attractiveness correlated with teachers' negative predictions about the children's future behavior and academic success. Clearly, teachers hold powerful positions and, as a result, have an important influence on the children's achievement.

The self-fulfilling prophecy effect that follows teachers' expectations can affect the opportunities of Hispanic students. First, the lack of understanding on the part of teachers denies equal education opportunity to Hispanic children, not only in the area of academic achievement but also in the area of affective development. Therefore, it is probable that the most serious harm that comes to the Hispanic child in school is the psychological damage of being misunderstood and rejected by insensitive teachers and classmates.

Teachers' expectations also can have a direct effect on student learning by affecting student opportunities to learn. Differences in expectations lead to differences in what is taught, which in turn lead to differences in what is ultimately learned. Some teachers of minority children too often impose their own values as the only, or, at least, most appropriate, belief system. They influence their students to believe that the students' world outside of school is valueless and that their family, neighbors, and communities, somehow, are culturally worthless. While being led to believe that their speech, their dress, their food, their customs, and their values are not acceptable, the students learn that they themselves are not acceptable.

Teachers do not expect Hispanic children, or minority children as a group, to excel in school. Faulty teacher perceptions appear to cause disadvantages to ethnic students. Findings indicate that these perceptions result in a lower achievement status for the students prior to the teacher's acquiring any objective knowledge. The lack of a high level of expectation continues to hurt these children psychologically and deprive them of an opportunity to advance educationally, economically, and socially in our country. The school experience should enhance the students' place in American society rather than become a negative experience. We must not assume that all Hispanic children are alike. They should not be mislabeled and placed in remedial classes or special education. In Texas, Hispanic children are overrepresented by 300 % in special education programs under the disabilities classification. The negative experiences that Hispanic students encounter predispose them to a higher rate of development of mental illness and/or emotional disturbances, such as depression, stress disorders, and low self-esteem. There is a real danger that the schools will unconsciously bring about personality disorganization in these children.

Another issue of great importance relates to the dual roles that Hispanic children are playing. They live double lives, existing in double-bind situations. Family atmosphere and values are in conflict with the school environment and Caucasian values. By the time they reach middle school, Hispanic students often choose to drop out rather than assimilate into an educational system that treats them as inferior.

More systematic research is needed to examine teachers' expectations and the double life expectations that are being imposed on Hispanic children. In order to develop insight and awareness to counteract the negative expectations of teachers, it is recommended that boards of education, community groups, district administrators, and government agencies make a commitment to develop and implement programs that are sensitive to the needs of Hispanic children.

Teachers need to be trained and made more aware of the vast influence that their attitudes and prejudices have on their pupils. As we see more and more children from the Hispanic culture who were born or now reside in our nation, this cannot be stressed enough. In the long run, the payoff is tremendous when we think of the benefits in terms of happier, more functional, and more productive citizens.

## IMPACT OF EXPECTATIONS ON CHILDREN'S PHYSICAL ACTIVITY

### Contributor: Dr. Roger L. Sweeting, Associate Professor (Emeritus)

Dr. Sweeting's academic preparation includes degrees in health and/or physical education from Bowling Green State University (B.S.), Pennsylvania State University (M.S.), and the University of Illinois (Ph.D.). He has more than 30 years of experience in higher education, including teaching physical education and health education (undergraduate and graduate), coaching varsity teams in basketball, baseball, and soccer, and administering academic and athletic programs. He has authored two books, a teaching guide, and numerous articles for professional journals. In addition, he has been active in faculty governance at the college and university levels and has held leadership positions in professional organizations at the state and national levels. Dr. Sweeting was the recipient of The Behrend College Teaching Excellence in Teaching award in 1984. He is an associate professor (emeritus) of health and physical education at The Pennsylvania State University.

### Testimonial

Most of my life has been spent teaching sports skills, both at the basic instructional and the varsity sports levels. At both levels, I have routinely observed the phenomenon of the self-fulfilling prophecy, with positive and negative connotations. Those who believe they are athletic tend to acquire skills quickly and delight in the process; those who have previously decided that they are not "natural athletes" are very slow to acquire new skills and may be reluctant even to try.

At the basic instruction level, each year brings a handful of students who believe that it is unfair for the University to impose a physical skills requirement on them, much less grade them on those skills. Often they believe that they cannot possibly compete with their "more athletic" classmates. Having committed themselves to a mind-set that does not envision the likelihood of success, they are usually not very successful.

Some students who enter the University are gifted mathematically, perhaps because they have had early and frequent exposure to mathematics and have diligently drilled to enhance those skills. Sometimes their talents are innate, but more often they are acquired. When we find a student who appears gifted in foreign languages, it is often because he or she has been reared in a bilingual or multilingual home and/or neighborhood. And just as often, our "natural" athletes have been similarly advantaged by early exposure rather than by latent talent, and have spent many hours acquiring those skills that make them appear to be naturals. As I see it, students without early exposure to math or foreign languages or sports can and do catch up if they receive adequate instruction and if they have not already doomed themselves to failure as a result of their willingness to succumb to a negative self-fulfilling prophecy. Students who are used to succeeding in a variety of pursuits, academic and otherwise, are most likely to assume that they will be successful in future endeavors, and that expectation also fulfills itself.

Two anecdotes, one from my teaching experiences and one from my coaching experiences, will serve to illustrate this point. The first involves a student who enrolled in a tennis class I was teaching at the college level. This person had decided years before that he was not athletic, so he proceeded to get out of all high school physical education classes; he was permitted to substitute band practice for PE, as was common in many high schools. Naturally, by the time I saw him he was far behind in the neuromuscular skills that were needed for tennis. Not only could he not serve or return serve with any dexterity, but he was unable to even drop a ball near his feet and contact it with his racquet after one bounce. He spent much time in class bemoaning the fact that he had not been blessed with the coordination of an athlete rather than focusing on the acquisition of new skills.

A few months later I went out for dinner at a fashionable restaurant, then stayed to dance to the music of a live band. And who do you suppose was playing percussion: base drum, snare drums, kettle drums, cymbals, marimbas, and shakers? Of course! It was that "uncoordinated" former student. Was he really uncoordinated? Of course not. I approached him during an intermission, to compliment him on his abilities, and we talked. I discovered that both of his parents were musicians, but neither had been interested in sports. Hence, as a child he acquired skills specific to their areas of interest but gradually fell behind other children in sports skills, to which he had not been exposed. As often happens, interest begets skill, skills inspire greater interest, and an upward spiral evolves. Likewise, lack of skill discourages interest, and the spiral leads downward instead. Learners often anticipate that success will follow earlier successes and that failure will follow previous failures—and they are frequently correct, not because of ability or inability, but because of that double-edged sword, positive or negative self-fulfilling prophecy.

The second anecdote, drawn from my basketball coaching days, clearly illustrates that the self-fulfilling prophecy can also be a positive influence. I had coached for five seasons with some success; the three most recent seasons had resulted in winning records and included a championship. We were returning a nucleus of good players, coupled with some fine incoming freshmen, which boded well for the season ahead. As had happened in each previous season, the opening week of practice brought with it a reporter from the student newspaper asking for an interview. I agreed, and he began to question me. One of his first questions was, "Well, Coach, how do you think your team will do this year?" My response, dangerously extemporaneous, was, "If we lose a game, I think it will be an upset." It wasn't until years later, tempered by the reality of harsh experience, that I realized what an audacious prediction I had made. At the time, I was merely giving an honest answer to an honest question. I had never been so bold in the past, and with good reason. But this was different: I knew my talent, I knew the schedule, and I was confident that we had a better than even chance against every opponent we would face.

Never mind that coaches aren't supposed to say such things for publication, fearing that rival coaches will put the quote on a bulletin board and use it in a pregame pep talk to convince our rivals that we don't respect them, that we are arrogant, and that we deserve a good whipping. I vaguely knew such things could happen, but I also knew that our student newspaper was unlikely to be read by anyone beyond our campus. More important, I knew that my own players would read what I had said and perhaps would be buoyed by the confidence I had expressed in them. And they were! That team won 20 games in succession and finished the regular season undefeated, thereby fulfilling my prophecy. It was the only undefeated season of my coaching career, which encompassed three sports and a total of 20 seasons. It was also the only time that I predicted an undefeated season, mostly because it was the only time that I truly believed that we might win every game. Was it a coincidence? I think not. I choose to believe that it is an illustration of how the self-fulfilling prophecy can work to advantage in competitive sports. Let it work for you.

There are dozens of less spectacular examples from my 30-plus years as an educator and coach. We have all known overachievers, and they are especially common in the athletic arena—people who succeed despite being "too small" or "too slow" or otherwise limited in potential. These individuals often find ways to compensate for their limited physical skills: desire and determination, superior conditioning and endurance, attention to detail, doing all the little things well. Those who have a keen mind and a stout heart can achieve beyond all reasonable expectations.

How else can you explain the presence of Jim Abbott in a major league baseball uniform, taking his regular turn as a starting pitcher? Jim was born with only one arm, and there is not much of a future for one-armed professional athletes, especially as big-league pitchers. But Jim Abbott believed he could overcome what he perceived to be a modest physical handicap. His career led him to success at the University of Michigan, to a gold medal on the U.S. Olympic team, and ultimately to the California Angels and the New York Yankees. His plan was to become a baseball player, and he fulfilled that self-prophecy.

These kinds of "miracles" also occur in our own teaching and coaching careers—if we permit and encourage them. Each student we work with, in a class or on a team, is a potential Jim Abbott in this sense: born with some limitations and blessed with some unique aspirations. One such student, missing an arm like Jim Abbott but with more modest athletic goals, enrolled in my tennis class determined to learn the sport. And she did! Together, we found a way. She became about as skilled as most beginning players I have taught, but she seemed to have more fun playing than most of them. Even the most limited of our students can experience the satisfaction of learning if we will do our part and help them find a way. I have concluded that it is a grievous error for a teacher or coach to assume that another person is incapable of fulfilling their own modest or lofty goals. Some dreams do come true.

## TEACHERS' DRESS AND ITS IMPACT ON STUDENTS' EXPECTATIONS

### Contributor: Bernard Davis, Member of Faculty of Education

Bernard Davis received his doctorate from the Massachusetts Institute of Technology in 1968, and has taught research methods in the Faculty of Education of Saint Mary's University, Halifax, Nova Scotia, since 1971. Each year his class selects a research question and designs and conducts a study to answer it. One of these assignments, the effect of teacher dress on the respect received from students, was the basis for the following testimonial.

### Testimonial

The study that resulted in the paper we published in the *Alberta Journal of Educational Research* (Davis, Clarke, Francis, MacMillan, McNeil, & Westhaver, 1992) began as I and 6 students enrolled in a graduate educational research seminar explored questions in education that puzzled us, seeking one we could answer through research. The one we finally fastened upon was a question of interest to a student who was also a junior high school principal. He enforced a dress code for teachers in his school and had always justified it by arguing that students give more respect to properly dressed teachers. But, as he admitted, he didn't know that this was true. We set out to determine whether it was.

Our literature search was, at the same time, enlightening and discouraging. It was enlightening in that we found experiment after experiment in which a person's dress affected how other people reacted. Proper dress allowed people to lead others across the street against the light, collect more—and more complete—interviews, get back a dime left in a phone booth, and avoid having their conversation in a university corridor interrupted.

But our literature search was disappointing in that we found no scale to measure respect, or its nearest behavioral equivalent, deference behavior. Leading hundreds of schoolchildren across the street against the light, soliciting their signatures on petitions, or having them walk between us or not walk between us wouldn't answer our question. Consequently, we did the work required to create a Likert scale to measure student expectation of deference behavior, validated it, and then gave it to 200 junior high school students. Half of the pupils saw at the top of the questionnaire a picture of a male teacher in a three-piece business suit. The other half saw a picture of the same teacher in the same pose and setting, but in a T-shirt and jeans.

Our results were that students expected their friends to give more respect (show more deference behavior) to the formally dressed teacher. So we did answer the principal's question. Part of the initial impression created in students by a formally dressed teacher is that the teacher is seen as more likely to get respect.

From the exercise we learned two things. First, we learned that we can end the embarrassment of having to defend our actions on the basis of hypotheses that we don't know are true if we are willing to test them by doing research. Second, we learned that teacher dress does indeed affect students' initial expectations of a teacher, in our case their initial expectation of how their fellow students will respond to him or her.

The self-fulfilling prophecy can work for you. But it will only work if what you do causes the initial expectation you want. If you are a substitute teacher who has begun to think you should meet your next new class dressed in a leather jacket and jackboots and carrying a bullwhip, you might consider that it is not overtly threatening dress but rather a proper business suit that research has shown to increase expectations of respect and deference behavior.

## CONSTRUCTING SELFS AND OTHERS

### Contributor: Gloria Ladson-Billings, Associate Professor

Gloria Ladson-Billings is associate professor at the University of Wisconsin-Madison, where she specializes in social studies education, multicultural education, and teacher education. Since 1992 she has been Codirector of Teach for Diversity, a master's with elementary certification program, and also has conducted many teaching workshops in multiculturalism and culturally relevant pedagogy at universities in this country and abroad. Reviewer, lecturer, and writer of numerous journal articles and publications, Dr. Ladson-Billings also authored the book *The Dreamkeepers: Successful Teachers of African American Children* (1994). During the first 10 years of her education career, she was a teacher and consultant in science and social studies in the school district of Philadelphia.

### Testimonial

Typically, self-fulfilling prophecy literature discusses the ways that teachers' conceptions of students' abilities shape students' achievement and school-based performance. However, in this essay, I want to address the way that teachers' conceptions of themselves, as well as their conceptions of others, helps to delimit the possibilities for academic success for students. In the rush to implement a "multicultural" curriculum, many school programs focus on the otherness of students—how their difference might be tolerated and sometimes appreciated. Rarely are teachers asked to examine the cultural lenses through which they view the world. Their beliefs, values, and assumptions remain unquestioned and unchallenged.

An important question with which white teachers must challenge themselves is, What does it mean to be white in this society? As explained by McIntosh (1989), a careful analysis of this question should reveal that whites in the United States enjoy certain privileges merely because they are white. From the simple act of walking into a department store without being followed and watched to the more complex structural privilege of being accorded better access to loans and financing, the society operates differently for people of color and for whites.

Because of the way most of us structure our social relations, it is possible that many white teachers never find themselves in the presence of African Americans or other people of color outside of the school. Thus they may not realize the dailyness of racism. My own white teacher education students who have African-American friends tell chilling tales of the differential treatment they have witnessed their friends experiencing. One student explained how when she went to "hang out" in the shopping malls with white friends, she experienced total freedom and acceptance by mall security. However, when she tried to engage in the same activity with African-American friends, they were followed, stopped, and questioned.

But it is not merely the mundane activities of everyday living that are at issue here. How does being white privilege one in the classroom? Or, stated differently, how does being African-American disadvantage one in the classroom? White (middle-class) children are expected to do well in the classroom. When they do not, the problem is presumed to be located in the school setting. Perhaps the teaching methods or materials need to be changed. Perhaps there is a personality conflict between the teacher and student. Whatever the problem, it must be remedied to ensure that the expectations for success are met.

Conversely, African-American students are not expected to achieve in the classroom. Those who achieve are thought to be anomalies—exceptions that defy the rule. African-American failure is thought to be located within the child and/or family. The marital or income status, morals, or beliefs of the parents are believed to explain school failure for African-American students. Rather than consider changing schooling experiences, the remedy is to separate the student from the home influences.

What can investigating oneself do to challenge the existing schooling situation for African-American students? My responses here are purely anecdotal, but they do reveal some powerful transformations experienced by white teachers. For several years I have been challenging my white students to interrogate their culture. The initial response of many is that they did not know much about their culture. Their halfhearted attempts discuss ethnic identity—participation in ethnic festivals, celebrations, and family rituals. However, those who bravely grapple with the concept of whiteness produce what they describe as "life-changing" essays that investigate issues they never dared challenge, as the following essay excerpt demonstrates:

When given the suggestion to write a course paper describing my culture, I mentally fought the idea. An intriguing idea, but a strange one. I never think about my culture conceptually the way I think about Hmong culture, Middle Eastern culture, or African American culture—which was precisely the professor's point in proposing the assignment. I found my mind racing in a kind of blank panic, looking for clues to find definitive characteristics of my culture that were as obvious and identifiable as Hmong needlework, or pita bread, or jazz. "We" Americans (in the United States) are inundated and bombarded by white culture, and its presence is so familiar to white people that we never have to define what that culture is or means to us as white, how that culture makes us what we are, or why we never have to consciously talk about it in order to find our personal identity within it. Our identity comes with being part of it from the day we are born. *No one ever questions us about anything on the basis of our color* [emphasis added].

This woman's willingness to interrogate her own cultural identity is an important first step in understanding the impact of culture in the lives of cultural "others" and in developing an informed empathy that will assist her in developing high expectations for all students. As we work to construct more accurate views of ourselves, we cannot help but construct more accurate views of others. These more accurate views are essential in developing self-fulfilling prophecies of high achievement for all children.

## A TEACHER EDUCATOR'S VIEW OF THE SFP

### Contributor: Suzanne Perry-Loss, Associate Professor and Family Therapist

Suzanne Perry-Loss is a an associate professor on the faculty of Gannon University in the School of Education, where she is currently the director of graduate education and the director of the Undergraduate Field Placement program. She is a practicing family therapist, a clinical member of the Association for Marriage and Family Therapy, and a certified Family Life Educator. Her teaching has focused on child and life span development, human sexuality, family relationships, parenting education, and numerous other areas of education. She received her D.Ed. and M.S. Ed. from The Pennsylvania State University. She is married and the mother of three children.

### Testimonial

When I think of the concepts of the self-fulfilling prophecy and expectations for students in relationship to any aspect of education, teacher education, and classroom practice, my thoughts focus on my many years of experience with teaching and advising nontraditional students. I taught for many years at a small private college for women where the percentage of nontraditional women returning to education rose to 68% of the student body. There were numerous other colleges in the area, two of which were public and of much less cost to the student.  Despite the cost differential, however, many nontraditional students transferred to the women's college.  Although they were succeeding academically at the other institutions, they sought fulfillment of another need.  They had heard that they would be supported more than just financially at this college.  During the years that I taught there and since that time, many of these women have remained in touch with the faculty members who believed in them and had high expectations of them.

The profile of these students was that many had not completed high school or had performed poorly academically and socially while they were there.  Some had been teenage parents or were married and divorced.  Some were substance abusers coming back to school after rehabilitation treatment.  Some had chronic illnesses such as cerebral palsy or had other physically limiting or body-image differences.  Some were from inner-city ghettos and carried the scars of the experience of living in the culture of poverty and extreme racial prejudice.  A common theme among all these women was that they had experienced dysfunctional families of origin, dead-end jobs, dead-end relationships, and numerous failures that had beaten them down.  The common experience that they shared overwhelmingly was oppressive abuse—physical, sexual, and emotional.  They had taken on a belief system that they were not good persons and that they would fail again.

Many of the women had no support system in their lives except those staff and faculty at the college who believed in them and who took time to talk to them and listen to their stories.   These faculty and staff supported them in rewriting their stories class by class, day by day, with the goal that they learn to believe in themselves.  Universally, over the years they had incorporated a belief system of worthlessness and low self-esteem.  They believed that they were only followers, never capable of assuming leadership roles.  They also expressed the belief that they were less valuable than men, and they had no expectations that they were even worth the support of the men in their lives.

These women told me that what made the difference in their lives—what enabled them to succeed, to grow in self-esteem, to trust themselves to take on leadership roles, to put forth the effort to earn the 4.0 GPA's, to remain in college despite extremely negative odds—was the belief certain faculty had in them as individuals. The repeated statements, "You *can* do it!" and "You *are* doing it!" began to change a negative self-fulfilling prophecy to one of believing in themselves as competent, worthwhile persons.  The faculty formed genuine caring relationships with these students, and that is what made the difference.  The teachers who made the difference were male and female, and they gave a very precious resource to their students—quality time.

The ultimate proof to me of an internalized, positive self-fulfilling prophecy was when the students in question began providing peer support for new nontraditional students who believed they were doomed to failure.  The group who had found their own sense of themselves told the newer students that they could do it too.  What these students keep telling those of us who supported them is, "Yes, I did it. I did the work, I earned the excellent grades, but you people believed in me. You genuinely cared about me as an individual. You were a role model for me. You were committed to me. You provided me with a holistic experience that affected every part of my life. Thank you."

# CHAPTER 16

# ERIC AND THE SFP

## INTRODUCTION

Chapter 16 does what all books on theory and practice in education should do. It introduces the reader to ERIC (Educational Resources Information Center), a readily available information and dissemination system that educators can use to learn still more about the theory and practice surrounding the self-fulfilling prophecy. No one book, not even this one, can present all the relevant information about any single topic. ERIC, as well as other information dissemination systems, is a must for today's decision-maker educators.

## WHAT IS ERIC?

ERIC, an acronym for Educational Resources Information Center, is an information system that is available worldwide. It is sponsored by the National Institute of Education within the U.S. Department of Education. ERIC is "one of the most important, if not the most important resource that has helped educators bridge the gap between practice and theory" (Barron, 1990, p. 47).

ERIC is dedicated to the progress of education through the dissemination of education research results, practitioner-related materials, and other resource information that can be used in developing more effective educational programs. Being decentralized, it is composed of sixteen clearinghouses, each responsible for obtaining, evaluating, abstracting, and disseminating information in a specific field of education.

The sixteen clearinghouses are shown in Figure 16.1, ERIC Clearinghouses. One or more of these clearinghouses probably has just the practitioner-related information that you are seeking.

**Figure 16.1**
**ERIC Clearinghouses**

**Adult, Career, and Vocational**
Ohio State University
Center for Research in Vocational
  Education
1900 Kenny Road
Columbus, Ohio 43210-1090
(614) 292-4353
(800) 848-4815

**Assessment and Evaluation**
Catholic University of America
209 O'Boyle Hall
Washington, DC 20064-3893
(202) 319-5120
(800) 464-3742

**Community Colleges**
University of California at Los Angeles
Mathematical Sciences Building
Room 8118
405 Hilgard Avenue
Los Angeles, California 90024-1564
(310) 825-3931
(800) 832-8256

**Counseling and Student Services**
Curry Building
University of North Carolina, Greensboro
1000 Spring Garden Street
Greensboro, NC 27412-5001
(919) 334-5100
(800) 414-9769

**Disabilities and Gifted Education**
Council for Exceptional Children
1920 Association Drive
Reston, Virginia 22091-1589
(703) 620-3660
(800) 328-0272

**Educational Management**
University of Oregon
1787 Agate Street
Eugene, Oregon 97403-5207
(503) 346-5043
(800) 438-8841

**Elementary and Early Childhood
Education**
University of Illinois
805 West Pennsylvania Avenue
Urbana, Illinois 61801-4897
(217) 333-1386
(800) 583-4135

**Higher Education**
George Washington University
One Dupont Circle, N.W., Suite 630
Washington, DC 20036-1183
(202) 296-2597
(800) 773-3742

**Information and Technology**
Syracuse University
Huntington Hall, Room 030
Syracuse, New York 13244-2340
(315) 443-3640
(800) 464-9107

**Languages and Linguistics**
Center for Applied Linguistics
1118 22nd St., N.W.
Washington, DC 20037-0037
(202) 429-9551
(800) 276-9834

**Reading, English, and Communication**
Indiana University
Smith Research Center, Suite 150
2805 East 10th Street
Bloomington, Indiana 47408-2373
(812) 855-5847
(800) 759-4723

**Rural Education and Small Schools**
Appalachia Educational Laboratory
1031 Quarrier Street
P.O. Box 1348
Charleston, West Virginia 25325-1348
(304) 347-0400
(800) 624-9120

**Figure 16.1**
**ERIC Clearinghouses (Continued)**

**Science, Mathematics, and**
**Environmental Education**
1929 Kenny Road
Columbus, Ohio 43210-1080
(614) 292-6717
(800) 276-0462

**Social Studies/Social Science Education**
Indiana University
Social Studies Development Center,
Suite 120
2805 East 10th Street
Bloomington, Indiana 47405-2373
(812) 855-3838
(800) 266-3815

**Teaching and Teacher Education**
American Association of Colleges for
Teacher Education
One Dupont Circle, N.W., Suite 610
Washington, DC 20036-1186
(202) 293-2450
(800) 822-9229

**Urban Education**
Teachers College, Columbia University
Institute for Urban and Minority
Education
Main Hall, Room 300, Box 40
525 West 120th Street
New York, New York 10027-9998
(212) 678-3433
(800) 601-4868

## Access to ERIC

Access to ERIC materials is made through one of two paper indexes, *Resources In Education* (*RIE*) and *Current Index to Journals in Education* (*CIJE*), as well as through on-line computer-retrieval systems. The indexes and, now more often the on-line computer-retrieval systems, are available in most college or university libraries, state departments of education, and larger school districts, and in some public libraries.

*Resources In Education*

As with the *R* in ERIC, the *R* in *RIE* stands for "Resources," not "Research." This is an especially important point for those who might dismiss ERIC as being useful only for researchers, not practitioners. *RIE* is a monthly journal that abstracts, indexes, announces, and provides a procedure to access "fugitive," or hard-to-get documents. These nonjournal documents, such as conference proceedings, speeches, curriculum guides, and project reports, are not normally available through library channels. Prior to *RIE*, the only way one was aware of such documents was to have personally attended the conference or heard the speech, or to know someone who had an extra copy of the desired curriculum guide or report. This hit-or-miss process severely limited one's access to information in the past. Not so now!

To use *RIE*, the first step is to look up the topic in the Subject Index or Author Index. Once an appropriate title is identified (for example, "Career Planning for Women"; see Figure 16.2, *RIE* Sample Resume) make note of the accompanying six-digit identifying ED (ERIC Document) number. In this instance, the number would be ED 654-321. Documents are also catalogued by

**Figure 16.2**
*RIE* Sample Resume

---

ED353377
The Self-Fulfilling Prophecy: Implications for the
Training/Learning Process.
Campbell, Clifton P.; Simpson, Charles R.
1992

63p.
EDRS Price - MF01 / PC03 Plus Postage.
Language: English
Document Type: TEACHING GUIDE (052)
Geographic Source: U.S.; Tennessee
Journal Announcement: RIEJUN93
         Target Audience; Teachers; Practitioners
This packet contains 27 transparency masters and a
script for instructor presentation of a 1-hour workshop
on the Pygmalion effect in training. It is aimed at
trainers as well as classroom teachers. The focus of the
guide is on how trainers'/teachers' behavior toward
students influences the outcome of training, with high
expectations leading to high performance and vice versa.
Materials include an outline of instruction (which
functions as a suggested script of presenter comments),
suggestions for instructor activities, and 13 references.
Some of the transparency topics are the Pygmalion
mythology, modern behavioral science, social and
psychological processes, ways to enhance student
performance, statements that erode student confidence,
and using mental imagery. (KC)
         Descriptors: Postsecondary Education; *Self
Fulfilling Prophecies; *Staff Development; *Student
Motivation; *Teacher Expectations of Students;
*Teacher Influence; Teaching Methods; *Training;
Transparencies; Workshops
         Identifiers: *Pygmalion

---

institution and publication type.  As titles can often be misleading, the second step is to turn to the Resume portion of the same index, use the six-digit ED number, and locate the appropriate Resume (detailed abstract).

As shown in the *RIE* Sample Resume (Figure 16.2), much information is provided, including author, origin of the document, publication type, descriptive note, key descriptors, and, most important, a rather lengthy informative abstract. Content experts at ERIC clearinghouses actually read each document in order to prepare these abstracts.  This saves users like you and me a whole lot of time, effort, and—possibly—disappointment in ordering something that ends up being nothing like what we thought it was going to be.  Often the detailed abstracts alone contain enough information to help educators make decisions.

If an identified document appears to be just what you are looking for, follow the simple directions provided in the *RIE* index to secure a microfiche (or paper) copy of the entire document.  Note, if microfiche are obtained directly from ERIC, they cost about one dollar per microfiche, each of which can hold up to 96 pages of print.  A more common method of getting a desired document on microfiche is to obtain it from a government-sponsored ERIC microfiche collection depository (usually based, or at least available, through college and university libraries).  These microfiche collections ensure that a document will never go out of print.

*RIE* documents go through a quality screening process by reviewers who, typically, have terminal degrees in their field and have a decade or more experience with ERIC.  They apply selection standards similar to those used for refereed journals in order to decide what is worth announcing in *RIE*.  If you were to scan the references listed at the end of this book, you would find that many of them carry an ED six-digit number indicating, that they were located by using ERIC's *RIE*.

*Current Index to Journals in Education*

*CIJE* includes articles from over 780 education periodicals, ranging from the most popular United States practitioner-oriented journals to British, Canadian, and Australian journals.  ERIC clearinghouses abstract, index, announce, and provide access to these journal articles.  It is like having an enormous library right at your fingertips!

To use *CIJE*, first look up the topic in the Subject Index.  Upon identifying an appropriate article, note its title, the journal in which it appears (name, volume, number, page), and the six-digit EJ (ERIC Journal) number.  The same information can be located by scanning *CIJE*'s Author Index or Journal Contents Index.  Using the latter is like walking up and down the aisles of a very large library, opening desired journals to examine their tables of contents.

As with the titles of *RIE* documents, the titles of journal articles do not always convey the real contents of the articles.  Why waste your time requesting and securing articles that may not be of use?  Instead, note the six-digit EJ number, turn to the Main Entry section, and locate the corresponding abstract. See the *CIJE* Sample Main Entry shown in Figure 16.3.  Key information

**Figure 16.3**
*CIJE* Sample Main Entry

---

EJ371734
**Black Dialect and Academic Success:  A Study of**
**Teacher Expectations.**
Cecil, Nancy Lee
Reading Improvement, v25 n1 p. 34–38 Spr 1988
Available From:  UMI
Language:  English
Document Type:  JOURNAL ARTICLE (080);  RESEARCH
REPORT (143)
Journal Announcement:  CIJOCT88


Compares teacher expectations for Black children who
speak Black Dialect with Black children who speak
Standard English.  Concludes that teachers expect
significantly greater overall academic achievement,
reading success, and intelligence from children who
speak Standard English.  (MM)
     Descriptors:  *Black Dialects; Black Education;
Black Stereotypes; *Black Students; Educational
Research; Elementary Education; Grade 2; Negative
Attitudes; Nonstandard Dialects; *Teacher Attitudes;
Teacher Behavior; Teacher Response; Teacher Student
Relationship
     Identifiers:  *Teacher Expectations

---

displayed includes a repeat of the article title and journal name, as well as author, Key Descriptors, and a one- or two-sentence abstract. This additional information, although considerably less than what is included in *RIE* abstracts, often clarifies whether or not an article is worth obtaining. Selected articles are usually accessible from nearby college libraries. Few, if any, resources are very far from your reach. The quality of articles identified and accessed through *CIJE* is ensured by the referee process inherent in most journal selection procedures.

## Sample RIE and/or CIJE Titles

Chapters 4 through 13 highlighted self-fulfilling prophecy research that related to selected human characteristics—gender, race, attractiveness, body build, and others. Much of this research was located by using ERIC. What follows are just a few more titles that deal with the SFP and still other human characteristics not covered in chapters 4–13. You may wish to use ERIC to investigate one or more of these topics. The key descriptor, "expectations," is used to access these titles.

Baskett, L. M. (1985). Sibling status effects: Adult expectations.

Carter, P. (1993). Effects of student age upon college teacher attitudes and teacher expectations of student achievement.

Durden, K. A. (1981). Teacher expectation as a moderator in student achievement and attitude formation in beginning typewriting.

Harkins, W. (1987). "Higher expectations" in the Catholic inner city high school.

Huebner, E. S. (1985). The influence of rural vs. non-rural background and setting variables on expectations.

Lankard, B. A. (1994). Employers' expectations of vocational education.

Levine, E. R. (1981). Teachers' academic and psycho-social expectations for children from single-parent families.

Newman, J. M. (1983). An analysis of teachers' expectations of children living with their divorced mothers.

O'Sullivan, M., and Dyson, B. (1994). Rules, routines, and expectations of 11 high school physical education teachers.

Rey, Y. M. (1985). Student perceptions of teacher expectations as expressed by differential teacher treatment in reading classes.

Workman, J. E., and Johnson, K. K. P. (1994). Effects of conformity and nonconformity to gender-role expectations for dress: Teachers versus students.

Still other human characteristics/self-fulfilling prophecy relationships, and there are many, that you could investigate are "left-handers versus right-handers," "red heads versus blondes," "students who use lots of makeup versus those who use little or no makeup," "people who prefer Coke versus those who prefer Pepsi," "students who prefer writing with pens versus those who prefer using pencils," and "cappuccino drinkers versus non-cappuccino drinkers." Surely, somewhere, sometime, someone has formed expectations about another person based upon one or more of these human characteristics. Note, I actually know of an administrator who commented that he or she expected such-and-such job candidate to be better than another candidate because the former candidate accepted a cup of cappuccino when it was offered while the latter candidate turned down the cup of cappuccino.

And then there is the expectations-related story told to me by one of my students. This student recently was stopped by our campus police for going through a stop sign. She immediately switched the car radio station from hard rock to classical music on WQLN, our public broadcasting station, in hopes of creating a better set of expectations in the mind of the approaching policeman. Did her expectations-related strategy work? Well, she did not receive a ticket. Of course, no one knows for sure if her strategy worked or not, but one thing that is for sure, if she is stopped again, she will immediately switch the radio station to WQLN.

### Thesaurus of ERIC Descriptors

One difficulty some busy practitioners have when looking up information is that they call what they are looking for by one name, but the index they are using calls it something else. To alleviate this problem, ERIC publishes a *Thesaurus of ERIC Descriptors*. It is normally found on the reference shelf just next to the *RIE* and *CIJE* indexes. The ERIC *Thesaurus* is a controlled vocabulary of educational terms called descriptors. They are used to index and enter documents into the ERIC system and to assist users—just like you—in searching the system. A user might look up the term "expectation" only to find related terms such as "achievement," "aptitude," "evaluation," "failure," "performance," "prediction," "stereotypes," and "success." Any of these descriptors may help you to unlock the specific information regarding the self-fulfilling prophecy that you are seeking. A couple of minutes work with the *Thesaurus* pays great dividends when undertaking a search for information.

### Computer-Search Capability

Thus far what has been described is a hands-on search of the two ERIC indexes, a process available to all educators. Today's CD-ROM (Read Only Menu) technology (e.g., DIALOG and SilverPlatter) now enables educators to conduct an on-line (on-screen, menu-driven) computer search of ERIC, entering key descriptors and allowing the computer to do the clerical work of sorting through documents. DIALOG, for instance, supplies ERIC on two CD-ROMs—one covering the time period 1966 to 1979 and one (updated periodically) covering the period from 1980 until the present (Bane & Tanner, 1989).

A computer's potential is evident when doing a Boolean search—using the AND, OR, and NOT logic functions. The AND narrows a search, the OR broadens a search, and the NOT reduces a group of titles (Purcell, 1989). For instance, if a topic under investigation has several aspects, for example, "expectations," "special education," and "secondary school," all three can be combined with the AND function so that only bibliographic citations with all three descriptors will be highlighted.

The end result of an on-line search is a bibliography of sources for your perusal. Most on-line computer-search technology also makes a printer available so that one can instantly produce a hard copy of desired resources. According to Dunman, "The ERIC system is a valuable resource for any educator, and on-line searching makes it more accessible than ever before" (1988, p. 47). The first time that you use ERIC, you will say "Wow! Where has this wonderful resource been all of my life?" Your expectations regarding doing research will become more positive.

### Warning!  Prepare a "Shopping List"

Most people know what happens when they are hungry and go grocery shopping without a list. They come home with a lot more than they went for. The same is true when an information-hungry person uses ERIC's *RIE* or *CIJE*. As you scan an ERIC Subject Index, you end up spotting interesting and useful resources outside your primary area of investigation. If you want to avoid this situation, prepare an investigative shopping list beforehand. Then again, why not let your imagination and your newfound information retrieval system run wild?

### Become an ERIC Contributor

Who are these people who publish in ERIC, especially in *RIE*? Who designs the curriculum guides, the tests, the position papers, and other useful practitioner-related resources announced in *RIE*? Who conducts and then writes up the successful projects (i.e., self-fulfilling prophecy projects) that are reported? Who reports on successful programs for bringing important concepts such as the self-fulfilling prophecy under control? People just like you! Yes, people just like you publish in ERIC—especially in *RIE*. In most schools, including yours, exciting things are happening that really ought to be shared with other educators. ERIC's *RIE* is just the vehicle for that sharing. The simple guidelines for doing this are described in *Submitting Documents to ERIC*, which is listed later under Resource Publications.

## CONCLUSION

There is simply not enough space in a chapter this length to describe fully the workings of ERIC and its potential to serve educators. What I hope to have done is to spark your interest in using ERIC as a tool to acquire the information so often requisite to successful problem solving. Quite bluntly, no other single information cataloging, indexing, and retrieval source exists that can match ERIC. For educators facing problem situations, ERIC enables them to access useful information quickly.

As a concerned educator, consider scheduling (or asking to have scheduled) an in-service program on ERIC. Acquire copies of the following resource publications, identify the closest library with the *RIE* and *CIJE* indexes and/or CD-ROM search facilities, and clarify the specific process faculty would use to acquire microfiche and/or paper copies of requested information. Pick out a problem in education—especially the self-fulfilling prophecy—and put ERIC to work for you and your colleagues.

## RESOURCE PUBLICATIONS

The publications listed here are available, free of charge, from the ERIC Processing and Reference Facility, 4350 East-West Highway, Suite 1100, Bethesda, Maryland 20814-4475. They include:

*A Pocket Guide to ERIC*
*Submitting Documents to ERIC*
*How to Use ERIC*

You also may phone a toll-free number, 1-800-USE-ERIC, to get on the mailing list of Access ERIC, a new system component that helps to disseminate ERIC products. Another source, *All About ERIC*, is available from the U.S. Government Printing Office, Washington, D.C. 20402.

# BIBLIOGRAPHY

Adams, G. R. (1977). Physical attractiveness, personality, and social reactions to peer pressure. *The Journal of Psychology, 96*, 287–296.

Adams, G. R. (1978). Racial membership and physical attractiveness effects on preschool teachers' expectations. *Child Study Journal, 8* (1), 29–41.

Adams, G. R., and Cohen, A. S. (1974). Children's physical and interpersonal characteristics that affect student-teacher interactions. *The Journal of Experimental Education, 43* (1), 1–5.

Adams, G. R., and Crane, P. (1980). An assessment of parents' and teachers' expectations of preschool children's social preference for attractive or unattractive children and adults. *Child Development, 51*, 224–231.

Adams, G. R., and Crossman, S. M. (1978). *Physical attractiveness: A cultural imperative*. Roslyn Heights, NY: Libra.

Adams, G. R., and LaVoie, J. C. (1974). The effects of student's sex, conduct, and facial attractiveness on teacher expectancy. *Education, 95* (1), 76–83.

Allington, R. (1980). Teacher interruption behaviors during primary-grade oral reading. *Journal of Educational Psychology, 72*, 371–377.

Aloia, G. F., and Aloia, S. D. (1982). Variations in expectations of the mainstreamed handicapped child by regular and special education teachers. *Journal for Special Educators, 19* (1), 13–19.

Aloia, G. F., and MacMillan, D. L. (1983). Influence of the EMR label on initial expectations of regular-classroom teachers. *American Journal of Mental Deficiency, 88* (3), 255–262.

Andersen, C. P. (1977). *Name game*. New York: Simon & Schuster.

Arganbright, J. L. (1983). Teacher expectations: A critical factor for student achievement. *NASSP Bulletin, 67* (64), 93–95.

Athanasiou, R., and Green, R. (1973). Physical attractiveness and helping behavior. *Proceedings of the 81st Annual Convention of the American Psychological Association* (pp. 289–290).

Babad, E. Y. (1985). Some correlates of teachers' expectancy bias. *American Educational Research Journal, 22* (2), 175–183.

Babad, E., Inbar, J., and Rosenthal, R. (1982). Pygmalion, Galatea, and the Golem:

Investigations of biased and unbiased teachers. *Journal of Educational Psychology, 74,* 59–474.

Babad, E., and Taylor, P. T. (1992). Transparency of teacher expectancies across language, cultural boundaries. *Journal of Educational Research, 86* (2), 120–125.

Bamburg, J. D. (1994). *Raising expectations to improve student learning.* Urban Monograph Series. Oak Brook, IL: North Central Regional Educational Laboratory.

Bane, R. K., and Tanner, D. F. (1989). Databases on CD-ROM: A tale of two ERIC's. *T.H.E. Journal, 16* (9), 51–59.

Banks, J. A., and Banks, C. A. (1993). *Multicultural education: Issues and perspectives.* Boston, MA: Allyn and Bacon.

Bannai, H. (1980). *Teachers' perceptions of comparisons between the spoken communication competencies of Asian American and Caucasian students* [CD-ROM]. Abstract from: ProQuest File: Dissertation Abstracts Item: No number cited

Barron, D. D. (1990). ERIC, research and online update. *School Library Media Activities Monthly, 7* (3), 46–50.

Bar-Tal, D., and Saxe, L. (1976). Physical attractiveness and its relationship to sex-role stereotyping. *Sex Roles, 2* (2), 123–133.

Beady, C., and Hansell, S. (1981). Teacher race and expectations for student achievement. *American Educational Research Journal, 18* (2), 191–206.

Bell, C. D., and Roach, P. B. (1986). A new problem for educators: Identification of the non-achieving gifted student. *Education, 107,* 178–181.

Bennett, R. E., Gottesman, R. L., Rock, D. A., and Cerullo, F. (1993). Influence of behavior perceptions and gender on teachers' judgments of students' academic skill. *Journal of Educational Psychology, 85* (1), 347–356.

Benson, P. L., Karabenick, S. A., and Lerner, R. M. (1976). Pretty pleases: The effects of physical attractiveness, race, and sex on receiving help. *Journal of Experimental Social Psychology, 12,* 409–415.

Blanck, P. D., and Rosenthal, R. (1984). Mediation of interpersonal expectancy effects: Counselor's tone of voice. *Journal of Educational Psychology, 6* (3), 418–426.

Blease, D. (1983). Teacher expectations and the self-fulfilling prophecy. *Educational Studies, 9* (2), 123–129.

Bloom, B. S. (Ed.). (1956). *Taxonomy of educational objectives. Handbook I: Cognitive domain.* New York: McKay.

Bloom, G. M. (1991). *The effects of speech style and skin color on bilingual teaching candidates' and bilingual teachers' attitudes towards Mexican-American pupils* [CD-ROM]. Abstract from: ProQuest File: Dissertation Abstracts Item: 9122517

Bonetati, D. (1994, April). *The effect of teachers' expectations on Mexican-American students.* Paper presented at the annual meeting of the American Educational Research Association, New Orleans, LA.

Bognar, C. J. (1982). Dissonant feedback about achievement and teachers' expectations. *Alberta Journal of Educational Research, 28* (3), 277–187.

Bognar, C. J. (1983). Teacher expectations and student characteristics. *Canadian Journal of Education, 8* (1), 47–56.

Bonner-Douglas, M. (1987). A study of positive impact of parents' and teachers' attitudes and expectations on poor, black students who are successful readers. *Journal of Clinical Reading, 2* (3), 7–10.

Bootzin, R. R., Bower, G. H., Zajonc, R. B., and Hall, E. G. *Psychology today: An introduction.* New York: Random House.

Boston, M. B. (1985). *Sex role models, implicit expectations, and sex typed behavior choice in 18 to 24 and 36 to 42 month old children* [CD-ROM]. Abstract from: ProQuest File: Dissertation Abstracts Item: 8500871

Boyce, C. K. (1990). *A study of teacher expectations regarding student achievement in low and high socioeconomic suburban elementary schools* [CD-ROM]. Abstract from: ProQuest File: Dissertation Abstracts Item: 9029124

Brantlinger, E. A. (1994). The social class embeddedness of middle school students' thinking about teachers. *Theory into Practice, 33* (3), 191–198.

Brattesani, K. A., Weinstein, R. S., and Marshall, H. H. (1984). Student perceptions of differential teacher treatment as moderators of teacher expectation effects. *Journal of Educational Psychology, 7* (2), 236–247.

Brehm, S. S., and Kassin, S. M. (1966). *Social psychology*. Boston, MA: Houghton Mifflin.

Brooks, T., and Marsh, E. (1981). *The complete directory to primetime network TV shows 1946-present*. New York: Ballantine Books.

Brophy, J. E. (1985). Teacher-student interaction. In J. Dusek (Ed.), *Teacher expectancies*. Hillsdale, NJ: Erlbaum.

Brophy, J. E., and Good, T. L. (1970). Teacher's communication of differential expectations for children's classroom performance: Some behavioral data. *Journal of Educational Psychology, 61,* 365–374.

Brophy, J. E., and Good, T. L. (1974). *Teacher-student relationships: Causes and consequences*. New York: Holt, Rinehart & Winston.

Brylinsky, J. A., and Moore, J. C. (1994). The identification of body build stereotypes in young children. *Journal of Research in Personality, 28,* 170–181.

Buchanan, B. A., and Bruning, J. L. (1971). Connotative meanings of first names and nicknames on three dimensions. *The Journal of Social Psychology, 85,* 143–144.

Butler-Por, N. (1989). *The phenomenon and treatment of academic underachievement in children of superior and average ability* [CD-ROM]. Abstract from: ProQuest File: Dissertation Abstracts Item: DX83415

Camaren, M. (1981). *Influence of ethnicity and perceptions of physical attractiveness on children's attributions of social behavior* [CD-ROM]. TN. Abstract from: ProQuest File: Dissertation Abstracts Item: 8101708

Campbell, C. P., and Simpson, C. R. (1992). *The self-fulfilling prophecy: Implications for the training/learning process* [Teaching guide]. (ERIC Document Reproduction No. ED 353 377)

Carter, R. R. (1981). *Exceptionality labels as a biasing factor in the perceptions of selected regular classroom teachers in North Carolina* [CD-ROM]. Abstract from: ProQuest File: Dissertation Abstracts Item: 8120347

Caskey, S. R., and Felker, D. W. (1971). Social stereotyping of female body image by elementary school age girls. *The Research Quarterly, 42* (3), 251–255.

Cavior, N., and Lombardi, D. A. (1973). Developmental aspects of judgment of physical attractiveness in children. *Developmental Psychology, 8* (1), 67–71.

Cecil, N. L. (1988). Black dialect and academic success: A study of teacher expectations. *Reading Improvement, 25* (1), 34–38.

Chaikin, A. L., Gillen, B., Derlega, V. J., Heinen, J.R.K., and Wilson, M. (1978). Students' reactions to teachers' physical attractiveness and nonverbal behavior: Two exploratory studies. *Psychology in the Schools, 15* (4), 588–595.

Chaikin, A. L., Sigler, E., and Derlega, V. J. (1974). Nonverbal mediators of teacher expectancy effects. *Journal of Personality and Social Psychology, 30,* 144–149.

Child, I. L. (1950). The relation of somatotype to self-rating on Sheldon's temperamental traits. *Journal of Personality, 18,* 440–453.

Christensen, L. M. (1990). Teaching Standard English: Whose standard? *English Journal, 79* (2), 36–40.

Claiborn, W. L. (1969). Expectancy effects in the classroom: A failure to replicate. *Journal of Educational Psychology, 60* (5), 377–383.

Clifford, M. M. (1975). Physical attractiveness and academic performance. *Child Study Journal, 5* (4), 201–209.

Clifford, M. M., and Walster, E. (1973). The effects of physical attractiveness on teacher expectation. *Sociology of Education, 46,* 248–258.

Clifton, R. A., and Bulcock, J. W. (1987). Ethnicity, teachers' expectations, and students' performance in Ontario schools. *Canadian Journal of Education, 12* (2), 294–315.

Clifton, R. A., Perry, R. P., Parsonson, K., and Hryniuk, S. (1986). Effects of ethnicity and sex on teachers' expectations of junior high school students. *Sociology of Education, 59* (1), 58–67.

Clinkenbeard, P. R. (1991). Unfair expectations: A pilot study of middle school students' comparisons of gifted and regular classes. *Journal for the Education of the Gifted, 15* (1), 56–63.

Cohn, T. (1987). *Multicultural teaching to combat racism in school and community.* Trentham, England: Trentham Books.

Collins, G. (1994, October 8). Kennedy vs. Romney: Old style liberalism vs. venture capitalism. *The Erie Times,* p. 3-B.

Collins, J. K., and Plahn, M. R. (1988). Recognition, accuracy, stereotypic preference, aversion, and subjective judgment of body appearance in adolescents and young adults. *Journal of Youth and Adolescence, 17* (4), 317–334.

Cooper H. M., and Tom, D. Y. H. (1984). Teacher expectation research: A review with implications for classroom instruction. *The Elementary School Journal, 85* (1), 77–89.

Cooper, M. A. (1989). *Factors associated with middle school "at risk" students in the regular classroom* [CD-ROM]. Abstract from: ProQuest File: Dissertation Abstracts Item: 8807956

Copper, M. C. (1990). *Teacher expectations and student achievement* [CD-ROM]. Abstract from: ProQuest File: Dissertation Abstracts Item: 9003625

Crano, W., and Mellon, P. (1978). Causal influences of teacher's expectations on children's academic performance: A cross-lagged panel analysis. *Journal of Educational Psychology, 70* (1), 39–49.

Crescimanno, R. (1982). *Culture, consciousness, and beyond.* Washington, DC: University Press of America.

Crumb, J. L. (1992). *Teacher and principal perceptions and student achievement in a Teacher Expectations and Student Achievement (TESA) program classroom* [CD-ROM]. Abstract from: ProQuest File: Dissertation Abstracts Item: No number available

Cullingford, C., and Morrison, J. (1995). Bullying as a formative influence: The relationship between the experience of school and community. *British Educational Research Journal, 21* (5), 547–560.

Daniell, B. (1984). Rodney and the teaching of standard English. *Language Arts, 61* (5), 498–504.

Dauber, S. (1987). *Sex differences on the SAT-M, SAT-V, TSWE, and ACT among college bound high school students.* Paper presented at the annual meeting of the American Educational Research Association, Washington, DC.

Davis, B., Clarke, A. R. B., Francis, J., MacMillan, J., McNeil, J., and Westhaver, P. (1992). Dress for respect: The effect of teacher dress on student expectations of deference behaviour. *The Alberta Journal of Educational Research, 38* (1), 27–31.

Deaux, K., and Lewis, L. L. (1984). Structure of gender stereotypes: Interrelationships among components and gender label. *Journal of Personality and Social Psychology, 46,* 991–1004.

Delcampo, D. S. (1983). *Ratings of preschool children from intact and divorced homes by preservice preschool teachers* [CD-ROM]. Abstract from: ProQuest File: Dissertation Abstracts Item: 8807956

Delgado-Contreras, C. (1985, March/April). *Teachers' expectations of bilingual children's achievement.* Paper presented at the annual meeting of the American Educational Research Association, Chicago, IL. (ERIC Document Reproduction No. ED 266 117)

Delgado-Gaitan, C., and Trueba, H. (1985). Ethnographic study of participant structures in task completion: Reinterpretation of "handicaps" in Mexican children. *Learning Disability Quarterly, 8,* 67–74.

DeMeis, D. K., and Turner, R. R. (1978). Effects of students' race, physical attractiveness and dialect on teachers' evaluations. *Contemporary Educational Psychology, 3,* 77–86.

Demetrulias, D. M. (1991). Teacher expectations and ethnic surnames. *Teacher Education Quarterly, 18* (2), 37–43.

Department of Education. (1990, October). *Academic performance. INAR/NACIE Joint Issues Sessions.* National Indian Education Association Annual Conference, San Diego, CA. (ERIC Document Reproduction No. ED 341 526)

Didham, C. K. (1990, February). *Equal opportunity in the classroom—Making teachers aware.* Paper presented at the annual meeting of the Association of Teacher Educators, Las Vegas, NV. (ERIC Document Reproduction No. ED 319 691)

Dion, K. K. (1973). Young children's stereotyping of facial attractiveness. *Developmental Psychology, 9,* 183–188.

Dion, K. K. (1974). Children's physical attractiveness and sex as determinants of adult punitiveness. *Developmental Psychology, 10* (5), 772–778.

Dion, K. K., and Berscheid, E. (1974). Physical attractiveness and peer perception among children. *Sociometry, 37* (1), 1–12.

Dion, K. K., Berscheid, E., and Walster, E. (1972). What is beautiful is good. *Journal of Personality and Social Psychology, 24* (3), 285–290.

Dunman, S. (1988). ERIC: An essential tool for educators. *Electronic Learning, 7* (4), 45–47.

Dusek, J. B. (1975). Do teachers bias children learning? *Review of Educational Research, 45* (4), 661–684.

Dusek, J. B., and O'Connell, E. J. (1973). Teacher expectancy effects on the achievement test performance of elementary school children. *Journal of Educational Psychology, 6,* 371–377.

Dvir, T., Eden, D., and Banjo, M. L. (1995). Self-fulfilling prophecy and gender: Can women be Pygmalion and Galatea? *Journal of Applied Psychology, 80* (2), 253–270.

Eden, D. (1984). Self-fulfilling prophecy as a management tool: Harnessing Pygmalion.

*Academy of Management Review, 9,* 64–73.

Eden, D. (1986). OD and self-fulfilling prophecy: Boosting productivity by raising expectations. *Journal of Applied Behavioral Sciences, 22,* 1–13.

Eden, D. (1988a). Creating expectation effects in OF: Applying self-fulfilling prophecy. *Research in Organizational Change and Development, 2,* 235–267.

Eden, D. (1988b). Pygmalion, goal setting, and expectancy: Compatible ways to boost productivity. *Academy of Managment Review, 13* (4), 639–652.

Eden, D. (1990a). Industrialization as a self-fulfilling prophecy: The role of expectations in development. *International Journal of Psychology, 25,* 871–886.

Eden, D. (1990b). *Pygmalion in management: Productivity as a self-fulfilling prophecy.* Lexington, MA: D. C. Heath.

Eden, D., and Ravid, G. (1981, December). *Effects of expectancy on performance among male and female trainees.* Paper presented at the International Interdisciplinary Congress on Women, Haifa, Israel.

Eden, D., and Ravid, G. (1982). Pygmalion vs. self-expectancy: Effects of instructor- and self-expectancy on trainee performance. *Organizational Behavior and Human Performance, 30,* 351–364.

Eden, D., and Shani, A. B. (1982). Pygmalion goes to boot camp: Expectancy, leadership, and trainee performance. *Journal of Applied Psychology, 67,* 194–199.

Elashoff, J., and Snow, R. (1971). *Pygmalion reconsidered.* Worthington, OH: Charles A. Jones.

Ellis, A., and Beechley, R. M. (1951). Emotional disturbance in children with peculiar given names. *Journal of Genetic Psychology, 85,* 337–339.

Evans, E. D., and Reiff, H. B. (1989). Undergraduate expectations and preferences toward working with students with handicaps. *College Student Journal, 23* (3), 206–213.

Feldman, R. S., and Prohaska, T. (1979). The student as Pygmalion: Effect of student expectation on the teacher. *Journal of Educational Psychology, 71* (4), 485–493.

Feldman, R. S., and Theiss, A. J. (1982). The teacher and student as Pygmalions: Joint effects of teacher and student expectations. *Journal of Educational Psychology, 74* (2), 217–223.

Felson, R. B. (1980). Physical attractiveness, grades and teachers' attributions of ability. *Representative Research in Social Psychology, 11,* 64–71.

Ferguson, A. M. (1982). A case for teaching Standard English to Black students. *English Journal, 71* (3), 38–40.

Firestone, G., and Brody, N. (1975). Longitudinal investigation of teacher-student interactions and their relationship to academic performance. *Journal of Educational Psychology, 67* (4), 544–550.

Flanders, N. A. (1969). Teacher effectiveness. In R. L. Ebel (Ed.), *Encyclopedia of educational research* (pp. 1423–1437). New York: Macmillan.

Fleming, E., and Anttonen, R. G. (1971). Teacher expectations or My Fair Lady. *American Educational Research Journal, 8,* 241–252.

Flugel, I. (1930). On the significance of names. *British Journal of Medical Psychology, 10,* 208–213.

Foil, D. G. (1980). *The effects of attitudes toward the handicapped and teacher expectancy due to assignment of the mentally retarded label on student performance* [CD-ROM]. Abstract from: ProQuest File: Dissertation Abstracts Item: 8021671

Follett, K. (1977). *Paper Money.* New York: Signet.

Ford, J. F. (1977). The prospective teacher and non-standard English: An attitudinal study. *English Education, 9* (1), 22–30.

Ford, M. E., Miura, I., and Masters, J. C. (1984). Effects of social stimulus value on academic achievement and social competence: A reconsideration of children's first-name characteristics. *Journal of Educational Psychology, 76* (6), 1149–1158.

Franzoi, S. L. (1996). *Social psychology.* Chicago: Brown & Benchmark.

Freeman, E. B. (1982). The Ann Arbor decision: The importance of teachers' attitudes toward language. *The Elementary School Journal, 83* (1), 41–47.

Freeman, J. (1983). Emotional problems of the gifted child. *Journal of Child Psychology and Psychiatry and Applied Disciplines, 24,* 481–485.

Frizzell, M. E. (1986). *Academic achievement expectations of handicapped and non-handicapped learners by vocation* [CD-ROM]. Abstract from: ProQuest File: Dissertation Abstracts Item: 8619110

Garwood, S. G. (1976). First name stereotypes as a factor in self-concept and school achievement. *Journal of Educational Psychology, 68* (4), 482–487.

Garwood, S. G., Cox, L., Kaplan, V., Wasserman, N, and Sulzer, J. L. (1980). Beauty is only "name" deep: The effect of first-name on rating of physical attraction. *Journal of Applied Social Psychology, 10,* 431–435.

Garwood, S. G., and McDavid, J. W. (1974, August/September). *Ethnic factors in stereotypes of given names.* Paper presented at the annual meeting of the American Psychological Association, New Orleans, LA.

Gault, A. (1989). *Mexican immigrant parents and the education of their handicapped children: Factors that influence involvement* [CD-ROM]. Abstract from: ProQuest File: Dissertation Abstracts Item: 8924819

Gilbert, S. I., and Gay, G. (1985). Improving the success in school of poor black children. *Phi Delta Kappan, 67* (2), 133–137.

Given, B. (1974). *Teacher expectancy and pupil performance: Their relation to verbal and non-verbal communications by teachers of learning disabled children* [CD-ROM]. Abstract from: ProQuest File: Dissertation Abstracts Item: 7419465

Gladding, S. T. (1982, March). *The name game: Community response to counselor names.* Paper presented at the annual convention of the American Personnel and Guidance Association, Detroit, MI.

Glasser, W. (1965). *Reality therapy.* New York: Harper & Row.

Glazzard, P. (1984). Are our expectations of special students high enough? *Teaching Exceptional Children, 16* (2), 136–139.

Goebel, B. L., and Cashen, V. M. (1979). Age, sex, and attractiveness as factors in student ratings of teachers: A developmental study. *Journal of Educational Psychology, 71* (5), 646–653.

Goldenberg, C. (1992). The limits of expectations: A case for case knowledge about teacher expectancy effects. *American Educational Research Journal, 29* (3), 517–544.

Good, T. L. (1982). How teachers' expectations affect results. *American Education, 18* (10), 25–32.

Good, T. L. (1984). *Making our schools more effective: Proceedings of three state conferences*[Research on teacher expectancies]. MO. (ERIC Document Reproduction No. ED 249 587)

Good, T. L. (1987). Two decades of research on teacher expectations: Findings and future directions. *Journal of Teacher Education, 38* (4), 32–47.

Good, T. L., and Brophy, J. E. (1978). *Looking in classrooms* (2nd ed.). New York:

Harper & Row.

Gore, D. A. (1981). *Sex-related differences in relation to teacher behavior as wait-time during fourth-grade mathematics* [CD-ROM]. Abstract from: ProQuest File: Dissertation Abstracts Item: 8127292

Gottfredson, D. C., Marciniak, E. M., Birdseye, A. T., and Gottfredson, G. D. (1995). Increasing teacher expectations for student achievement. *Journal of Educational Research, 88* (3), 155–163.

Granger, R. C., Mathews, M., Quay, L. C., and Verner, R. (1977). Teacher judgments of communication effectiveness of children using different speech patterns. *Journal of Educational Psychology, 69,* 793–796.

Gross, A., and Crofton, C. (1977). What is good is beautiful. *Sociometry, 40,* 85–90.

Guskin, J. T. (1970, March). *The social perception of language variations: Black and white teacher attitudes toward speakers of different racial and social class background.* Paper presented at the American Educational Association Conference, Minneapolis, MN.

Hackett, E. D., Mirvis, P. H., and Sales, A. L. (1991). Women's and men's expectations about the effects of new technology at work. *Group & Organization, 16* (1), 60–85.

Hassenpflug, A. (1994). Notes from an English teacher: In pursuit of great expectations. *Clearing House, 67* (3), 161–162.

Hall, E. G. (1983). Recognizing gifted underachievers. *Roeper Review, 5,* 23–25.

Hall, J. L. (1993). What can we expect from minority students? *Contemporary Education, 64* (3), 180–182.

Hanley, C. (1951). Physique and reputation of junior high boys. *Child Development, 22* (4), 247–260.

Hansell, S., Sparacino, J., and Ronchi, D. (1982). Physical attractiveness and blood pressure: Sex and age differences. *Personality and Social Psychology Bulletin, 8* (1), 113–121.

Harari, H., and McDavid, J. W. (1973). Name stereotypes and teachers' expectations. *Journal of Educational Psychology, 65* (2), 222–225.

Harris, J. J., II. (1990). *Evaluating the influence of TESA training on teacher behavior in the classroom* [CD-ROM]. Abstract from: ProQuest File: Dissertation Abstracts Item: 9028045

Hassenpflug, A. (1994). Notes from an English teacher: In pursuit of great expectations. *Clearing House, 67* (3), 161–162.

Haynes, N. M. (1981). *The influence of the self-fulfilling prophecy on the academic achievement and self-concept of black marginal college students* [CD-ROM]. Abstract from: ProQuest File: Dissertation Abstracts Item: 8122488

Heilman, M. E., and Saruwatari, L. R. (1979). When beauty is beastly: The effects of appearance and sex on evaluations of job applicants for managerial and nonmanagerial jobs. *Organizational Behavior and Human Performance, 23,* 360–372.

Hess, K. M. (1972). Is learning a standard English important? An overview. *The Florida FL Reporter, 10* (1/2), 39–42, 54.

Hindalong, R. L. (1993). *An analysis of the achievement of students with TESA-trained teachers compared to the achievement of students with non-TESA trained teachers* [CD-ROM]. Abstract from: ProQuest File: Dissertation Abstracts Item: 9322798

Hirsch, E. D. (1987). *Cultural literacy.* Boston, MA: Houghton Mifflin.

Hoge, R. D. (1984). The definition and measurement of teacher expectations: Problems and prospects. *Canadian Journal of Education, 9* (2), 213–228.

Horowitz, I. A., and Bordens, K. S. (1995). *Social psychology.* Mountain View, CA: Mayfield.

Hull, J. D. (1994, April 4). Do teachers punish according to race? *Time*, 30.

Humphreys, L. G. (1957). Characteristics of type concepts with special reference to Sheldon's typology. *Psychological Bulletin, 54* (3), 218–228.

Hunsberger, B., and Cavanagh, B. (1988). Physical attractiveness and children's expectations of potential teachers. *Psychology in the Schools, 25* (1), 70–74.

Hwang, U. L. (1993). *Wait-time as a variable in sex-related differences during computation and problem-solving instruction of third and sixth grades* [CD-ROM]. Abstract from: ProQuest File: Dissertation Abstracts Item: 9314568

Jackson, B. (1985). Lowered expectations: How schools reward incompetence. *Phi Delta Kappan, 67* (4), 304–305.

Janssen, B., and Whiting, H. T. A. (1984). Sheldon's physical-psychical typology revisited. *Journal of Research in Personality, 18*, 432–441.

Jensen, A. R. (1969). How much can we boost IQ and scholastic achievement? *Harvard Educational Review, 39*, 1–123.

Johnson, M. J. (1991). *American Indians and Alaska natives with disabilities* (Report No. 108612). In Indian Nations At Risk Task Force Commissioned Papers, Washington, D.C. (ERIC Document Reproduction No. 343 770)

Jones, S. C. (1990). *The effects of the Teacher Expectations and Student Achievement program (TESA) on the reading achievement and self-esteem of suburban high school students* [CD-ROM]. Abstract from: ProQuest File: Dissertation Abstracts Item: 9032902

Jungbluth, P. (1994). Teacher expectations and ethnicity: The educational and opportunities of adolescent migrants in the Netherlands. *Zeitschrift fur Padagogik, 40* (1), 113–125.

Jussim, L. (1989). Teacher expectations: Self-fulfilling prophecies, perceptual biases, and accuracy. *Journal of Personality and Social Psychology, 57* (3), 469–480.

Jussim, L. (1990). Social reality and social problems: The role of expectations. *Journal of Social Issues, 46*, 9–34.

Keas, S., and Beer, J. (1992). Stereotypes about women's body types associated with occupations. *Perceptual and Motor Skills, 75*, 223–230.

Kehle, T. J., Bramble, W. J., and Mason, E. J. (1974). Teachers' expectations: Ratings of student performance as biased by student characteristics. *The Journal of Experimental Education, 43* (1), 54–59.

Kenealy, P., Frude, N., and Shaw, W. (1988). Influence of children's physical attractiveness on teacher expectations. *The Journal of Social Psychology, 128* (3), 373–383.

King, A. S. (1971). Self-fulfilling prophecies in training the hard-core: Supervisors' expectations and the underprivileged workers' performance. *Social Science Quarterly, 52*, 369–378.

Kohler, P. L. (1987). *The effects of the Teacher Expectations and Student Achievement model on the achievement and self-concept of mildly handicapped students receiving resourceroom* [CD-ROM]. Abstract from: ProQuest File: Dissertation Abstracts Item: 8807956

Kolb, K. J., and Jussim, L. (1994). Teacher expectations and underachieving gifted children. *Roeper Review, 17* (1), 26–30.

Koster, J. J. (1987). *Effects of handicap labels, gender, mainstreaming experience and authoritarianism on academic and behavioral expectations of teachers* [CD-ROM]. Abstract from: ProQuest File: Dissertation Abstracts Item: 8714607

Kramer, L. R. (1986). Career awareness and personal development: A naturalistic study of gifted adolescent girls' concerns. *Adolescence, 21,* 123–131.

Langlois, J. H., and Roggman, L. A. (1990). Attractive faces are only average. *Psychological Science, 1 (2),* 115–121.

Langlois, J. H., and Stephan, C. (1977). The effects of physical attractiveness and ethnicity on children's behavioral attributions and peer preferences. *Child Development, 48,* 1694–1698.

Lawson, E. D. (1971). Semantic differential analysis of men's first names. *The Journal of Psychology, 78,* 229–240.

Lawson, E. D. (1991). *Psychological dimensions of women's names: A semantic differential analysis.* New York, NY. (ERIC Document Reproduction No. ED 343 409)

Lee-Corbin, H. (1994). Teacher expectations and the able child. *Early Child Development and Care, 98,* 73–78.

Lerner, R. M. (1969). Some female stereotypes of male body build-behavior relations. *Perceptual and Motor Skills, 28,* 363–366.

Lerner, R. M., and Korn, S. J. (1972). The development of body-build stereotypes in males. *Child Development, 43,* 908–920.

Lerner, R. M., and Lerner, J. V. (1977). Effects of age, sex, and physical attractiveness on child-peer relations, academic performance, and elementary school adjustment. *Developmental Psychology, 13* (6), 585–590.

Levine, M. B., and Willis, F. N. (1994). Public reactions to unusual names. *The Journal of Social Psychology, 134* (5), 561–568.

Light, R. L., Richard, D. P., and Bell, P. (1978). Development of children's attitudes toward speakers of standard and non-standard English. *Child Study Journal, 8* (4), 253–265.

Lindley, H. A., and Keithley, M. E. (1991). Gender expectations and student achievement. *Roper Review, 13* (4), 231–215.

Linehan, S. A., Brady, M. P., and Hwang, C. (1991). Ecological versus developmental assessment: Influences on instructional expectations. *Journal of the Association for Persons with Severe Handicaps, 16* (3), 146–153.

Loftus, P. (1992). The Pygmalion effect. *Canadian Banker, 99* (5), 34–37.

Loftus, P. (1995). Expect yourself. *Canadian Banker, 102* (1), 31–33.

Major, B., Vanderslice, V., and McFarlin, D. B. (1984). Effects of pay expected on pay received: The confirmatory nature of initial expectations. *Journal of Applied Social Psychology, 14* (5), 399–412.

Marcus, G., Gross, S., and Seefeldt, C. (1991). Black and white students' perceptions of teacher treatment. *Journal of Educational Research,* 84 (6), 363–367.

Marwit, K., Marwit, S., and Walker, E. (1978). Effects of student race and physical attractiveness on teachers' judgments of transgressions. *Journal of Educational Psychology, 70* (6), 911–915.

Masland, S. W. (1979). Black dialect and learning to read: What is the problem? *Journal of Teacher Education, 30* (2), 41–44.

McCluhan, M. (1964). *Understanding media.* New York: McGraw-Hill.

McConnell, J. H. (1985). *A study of the impact of an inservice teacher education program on teacher expectation on the behavior of the participating teachers and their designated target students* [CD-ROM]. Abstract from: ProQuest File: Dissertation Abstracts Item: 8505894

McCormick, T. E., and Noriega, T. (1986). Low versus high expectations: A review of teacher expectation effects on minority students. *Journal of Educational Equity and Leadership, 6* (3), 224–234.

McCullough, M. P. (1981). *Teachers' knowledge of and attitudes toward Black English and correction of dialect-related reading miscues* [CD-ROM]. Abstract from: ProQuest File: Dissertation Abstracts Item: 8204712

McDavid, J. W., and Harari, H. (1966). Stereotyping of names and popularity in grade-school children. *Child Development, 37,* 453–459.

McIntosh, P. (1989, Winter). White privilege: Unpacking the invisible knapsack. *Independent Schools,* 31–36.

Mehrabian, A., and Valdez, P. (1990). Basic name connotations and related sex stereotyping. *Psychological Reports, 66* (2), 1309–1310.

Mendels, G. G., and Flanders, J. P. (1973). Teachers' expectations and pupil performance. *American Educational Research Journal, 10,* 203–212.

Merton, R. K. (1948). The self-fulfilling prophecy. *Antioch Review, 8,* 193–210.

Merton, R. K. (1949). *Social theory and social structure.* New York: Free Press.

Metcalf, L. (1995). Great expectations. *Learning, 23* (5), 93–95.

Meza, A. (1986). *An identification of factors associated with the Hispanic student dropout* [CD-ROM]. Abstract from: ProQuest File: Dissertation Abstracts Item: 8624545

Michlin, M. L. (1977). *The effects of social perceptual and causal attributional variables on teachers' perceptions and ratings of students' written composition* [CD-ROM]. Abstract from: ProQuest File: Dissertation Abstracts Item: 8807956

Miller, A. G. (1970). Role of physical attractiveness in impression formation. *Psychometric Science, 19,* 241–243.

Miller, A. G. (1982). *In the eye of the beholder: Contemporary issues in stereotyping.* New York: Praeger.

Minner, S., and Prater, G. (1984). College teachers' expectations of LD students. *Academic Therapy, 20* (2), 225–229.

Mohd.Nor, A. K. B. (1990). *Characteristics of effective rural secondary schools in Malaysia* [CD-ROM]. Abstract from: ProQuest File: Dissertation Abstracts Item: 9009574

Monk, M. J. (1983). Teacher expectations? Pupil responses to teacher mediated classroom climate. *British Educational Research Journal, 9* (2), 153–166.

Moore, D. W. (1984). Disparate teacher attention favouring the more able: Some data from Papua New Guinean community and provincial high schools. *The Australian Journal of Education, 28* (2), 154–164.

Moore, H. A., and Johnson, D. R. (1983). A reexamination of elementary school teacher expectations: Evidence of sex and ethnic segmentation. *Social Science Quarterly, 64* (3), 460–475.

*Morning News* (1995, December 18). Barbie doll shortage frustrates consumers. (Erie, PA), pp. 1A, 2A.

Morrison, T. G., Bell, E. M., Morrison, M. A., Murray, C. A., and O'Connor, W. (1994). An examination of adolescents' salary expectations and gender-based occupational stereotyping. *Youth & Society, 26* (2), 178–193.

Murphy, W. F. (1957). A note on the significance of names. *Psychoanalytic Quarterly,*

*26,* 91–106.

Murray, C. B., and Clark, R. M. (1990). Targets of racism. *The American School Board Journal, 177* (6), 22–24.

Myers, D. G. (1996). *Social psychology.* New York: McGraw Hill.

Neuberg, S. L., Judice, T. N., Virdin, L. M., and Carrillo, M. A. (1993). Perceiver self-presentational goals as moderators of expectancy influences: Ingratiation and the disconformation of negative expectancies. *Journal of Personality and Social Psychology, 64* (3), 409–420.

Oakes, A. (1996, April 22). Labeling deprives you of the most fulfilling relationships. *Daily Collegian,* 11.

Oechsli, M. (1994). Pygmalion revisited. *Managers Magazine, 69* (3), 16–21.

Ogbu, J. U. (1978). *Minority education and the caste: The American system in cross-cultural perspective.* San Diego, CA: Academic Press.

Paine, G. A. (1981). *Ethnic, class, and role preferences for behavioral expectations for preschool* [CD-ROM]. Abstract from: ProQuest File: Dissertation Abstracts Item: 8029686

Palardy, J. M. (1969). What teachers believe—What children achieve. *Elementary School Journal, 69,* 370–374.

Paludi, M. A., and Strayer, L. A. (1985). What's in an author's name? Differential evaluations of performance as a function of author's name. *Sex Roles, 12* (3/4), 353–361.

Patriarca, L. A., and Kragt, D. M. (1986). Teacher expectations and student achievement: The ghost of Christmas future. *Curriculum Review, 25* (5–6), 48–50.

Peterson, M. A. (1989). *Evaluation of Teacher Expectations and Student Achievement* [CD-ROM]. Abstract from: ProQuest File: Dissertation Abstracts Item: 8909895

Pixton, W. H. (1974). Contemporary dilemma: The question of standard English. *College Composition and Communication, 25* (4), 247–253.

Politzer, R. L., and Hoover, M. R. (1976). *Teachers' and pupils' attitudes toward Black English speech varieties and black pupils' achievement.* Stanford, CA: Stanford Center for Research and Development in Teaching.

Price, E. S. (1985). *An investigation of the academic achievement of fifth grade students as it relates to social psychological climate in the classroom* [CD-ROM]. Abstract from: ProQuest File: Dissertation Abstracts Item: 8600534

*Publication manual of the American Psychological Association.* (1994). Washington, DC: American Psychological Association.

Pugh, L. G. (1974, April). *Teacher attitude and expectation associated with race and social class.* Paper presented at the annual meeting of the American Educational Research Association, Chicago, IL.

Purcell, R. (1989). Electronic ERIC. *Small Computers in Libraries, 8* (2), 18–21.

Ramirez, A. G., Arce-Torres, E., and Politzer, R. L. (1976). *Language attitudes and the achievement of bilingual pupils.* Stanford, CA: Stanford Center for Research and Development in Teaching.

Rampaul, W. E., Singh, M., and Didyk, J. (1984). The relationship between academic achievement and teacher expectations of native children in a northern Manitoba school. *TESL Canada Journal, 2* (1), 27–40.

Rappaport, M. M., and Rappaport, H. (1975). The other half of the expectancy equation: Pygmalion. *Journal of Educational Psychology, 67* (4), 531–536.

Research for Better Schools. (1987). Teacher expectations action packet. Research, strategies and programs for special populations. Philadelphia: Research for Better Schools. (ERIC Document Reproduction No. ED 289 830)

Rheem, H. (1995). Effective leadership: The Pygmalion effect. *Harvard Business Review, 73* (3), 14.

Rice, B. (1990). *High school teachers' perceptions of African-American male high school students in San Francisco* [CD-ROM]. Abstract from: ProQuest File: Dissertation Abstracts Item: 8926015

Rich, J. (1975). Effects of children's physical attractiveness on teachers' evaluations. *Journal of Educational Psychology, 67* (5), 599–609.

Richardson, R. C, Jr., and Skinner, E. F. (1992). Helping first-generation minority students achieve degrees. *New Directions for Community Colleges, 20* (4), 29–43.

Richey, L. S., and Yesseldyke, J. E. (1983). Teachers' expectations for the younger siblings of learning disabled students. *Journal of Learning Disabilities, 16* (10), 610–615.

Rist, R. C. (1970). Student social class and teacher expectations: The self-fulfilling prophecy in ghetto education. *Harvard Educational Review, 40,* 411–451.

Roach, T. D., and Arnold, V. D. (1991). Leadership: The power of expectations. *Business Education Forum, 46* (1), 40–42.

Robinson, J. (1983). *Social typing in Korean schools: The effects of differential teacher interactional style* [CD-ROM]. Abstract from: ProQuest File: Dissertation Abstracts Item: 8307204

Robinson, J. (1994). Social status and academic success in South Korea. *Comparative Education Review, 38* (4), 506–530.

Rolison, M. A., and Medway, F. J. (1985). Teachers' expectations and attributions for student achievement: Effects of label, performance pattern, and special education intervention. *American Educational Research Journal, 22* (4), 561–573.

Rosenthal, R. (1973a). The mediation of Pygmalion effects: A four-factor "theory." *Papua New Guinea Journal of Education, 9* (1), 1–12.

Rosenthal, R. (1973b). The Pygmalion effect lives. *Psychology Today, 7* (4), 56–60, 62–63.

Rosenthal, R. (1974). *On the social psychology of the self-fulfilling prophecy: Further evidence for Pygmalion effects and their mediating mechanisms.* New York: MSS Modular Publications.

Rosenthal, R. (1987). Pygmalion effects: Existence, magnitude, and social importance. *Educational Researcher, 16,* 37–41.

Rosenthal, R. (1989, August). *Experimenter expectancy, covert communication, and meta-analytic methods.* Paper presented at the annual meeting of the American Psychological Association, New Orleans, LA (ERIC Document Reproduction No. ED 317 551)

Rosenthal, R., and DePaulo, B. M. (1979). Expectancies, discrepancies, and courtesies in nonverbal communication. *The Western Journal of Speech Communication, 43,* 76–95.

Rosenthal, R., and Fode, K. L. (1963). The effects of experimenter bias on the performance of the albino rat. *Behavioral Science, 8,* 183–189.

Rosenthal, R., and Jacobson, L. (1966). Teachers' expectancies: Determinants of pupils' IQ gains. *Psychological Reports, 19,* 115–118.

Rosenthal, R., and Jacobson, L. (1968a). *Pygmalion in the classroom.* New York: Holt, Rinehart & Winston.

Rosenthal, R., and Jacobson, L. (1968b). Teacher expectations for the disadvantaged. *Scientific American, 218* (4), 19–23.

Rosenthal, R., and Lawson, R. (1964). A longitudinal study of the effects of experimenter bias on the operant learning of laboratory rats. *Journal of Psychiatric Research, 2,* 61–72.

Rosenthal, R., and Rubin, D. B. (1978). Interpersonal expectancy effects: The first 345 studies. *The Behavioral and Brain Sciences, 3* (1), 377–386.

Sadker, M., and Sadker, D. (1994). *Failing at fairness: How our schools cheat girls.* New York: Simon & Schuster.

Sakya, B. R. (1980). *Teacher expectation biases as affected by hereditary social structures in Nepal* [CD-ROM]. Abstract from: ProQuest File: Dissertation Abstracts Item: No number available

Saracho, O. N. (1991). Teacher expectations of students' performance: A review of the research. *Early Child Development and Care, 76,* 27–41.

Sato, C. J. (1989). A nonstandard approach to standard English. *TESOL Quarterly, 23* (2), 259–282.

Schleper, D. R. (1995). Well, what do you expect? *Perspectives in Education and Deafness, 13* (3), 2–3.

Schmuck, P. A., and Schmuck, R. A. (1994). Gender equity: A critical democratic component of America's high schools. *NASSP Bulletin, 78* (558), 22–31.

Shaw, W. C. (1981). The influence of children's dentofacial appearance on their social attractiveness as judged by peers and adults. *American Journal of Orthodonistry, 79,* 399–415.

Shaw, W. C., and Humphreys, S. (1982). Influence of children's dentofacial appearance on teacher expectations. *Community Dentistry and Oral Epidemiology, 10,* 313–319.

Sheldon, W. H. (1940). *The varieties of human physique: An introduction to constitutional psychology.* New York: Harper.

Sheldon, W. H. (1942). *The varieties of temperament: A psychology of constitutional temperament.* New York: Harper.

Sheldon, W. H. (1954). *Atlas of men: A guide for somatotyping the adult male at all ages.* New York: Harper.

Shepardson, D. P., and Pizzini, E. L. (1992). Gender bias in female elementary teachers' perceptions of the scientific ability of students. *Science Education, 76* (2), 147–152.

Shimko, B. W. (1989). Using positive Pygmalion to build your work force. *The Cornell H.R.A. Quarterly, 30* (3), 91–94.

Shimko, B. W. (1990). The McPygmalion effect. *Training & Development Journal, 44* (6), 64–70.

Smead, V. S. (1984). Self-fulfilling prophecies in the classroom: Dead end or promising beginning? *Alberta Journal of Educational Research, 30* (2), 146–156.

Smey-Richman, B. (1989). *Teacher expectations and low-achieving students.* Philadelphia: Research for Better Schools, (ERIC Accession No. ED 328 627).

Smith, E. R., and Mackie, D. M. (1995). *Social psychology.* New York: Worth.

Smith, F. J., and Luginbuhl, J. E. R. (1976). Inspecting expectancy: Some laboratory results of relevance for teacher training. *Journal of Educational Psychology, 68* (3), 265–272.

Smith, K. L. (1989, February). *Teacher expectations and minority achievements: A study of black students in Fairfax County.* Paper presented at the Eastern Educational Research Conference, Savannah, GA.

Snow, R. E. (1969). Unfinished Pygmalion. *Contemporary Psychology, 14*, 197–199.

Snyder, M., Tanke, E. D., and Berscheid, E. (1977). Social perception and interpersonal behavior: On the self-fulfilling nature of social stereotypes. *Journal of Personality and Social Psychology, 35* (9), 565–666.

Solomon, G. B., Wiegardt, P. A., Yusuf, F. R., Kosmitzki, C., Williams, J., Stevens, C. E., and Wayda, V. K. (1996). Expectancies and ethnicity: The self-fulfilling prophecy in college basketball. *Journal of Sport & Exercise Psychology, 18*, 83–88.

Sparacino, J., and Hansell, S. (1979). Physical attractiveness and academic performance: Beauty is not always talent. *Journal of Personality, 47*, 449–469.

Spillman, D. M., and Everington, C. (1989). Somatotypes revisited: Have the media changed our perception of the female body image? *Psychological Reports, 64*, 887–890.

Sprouse, J. L., and Webb, J. E. (1994). *The Pygmalion effect and its influence on the grading and gender assignment on spelling and essay assessments.* Master's thesis, University of Virginia. (ERIC Document Reproduction No. ED 374 096)

Staffieri, J. R. (1967). A study of social stereotype of body image in children. *Journal of Personality and Social Psychology, 7* (1), 101–104.

Stager, S., and Burke, P. (1982). A re-examination of body build stereotypes. *Journal of Research in Personality, 16*, 435–446.

Steele, K. M., and Smithwick, L. E. (1989). First names and first impressions: A fragile relationship. *Sex Roles, 21* (7/8), 517–523.

Stewart, F. K. (1993). Teacher attitudes and expectations regarding mainstreaming of handicapped children. *TEASE, 6* (1), 39–45.

St. George, A. (1983). Teacher expectations and perceptions of Polynesian and Pakeha pupils and the relationship to classroom behaviour and achievement. *British Journal of Educational Psychology, 53* (1), 48–59.

Styczynski, L. E., and Langlois, J. H. (1977). The effects of familiarity on behavioral stereotypes associated with physical attractiveness in young children. *Child Development, 48*, 1137–1141.

Sutton, C. D., and Woodman, R. W. (1989). *Pygmalion goes to work: The effects of supervisor expectations in a retail setting.* Unpublished doctoral dissertation, Texas A&M University, College Station.

Tal, Z., and Babad, E. (1989). The "teacher's pet" phenomenon as viewed by Israeli teachers and students. *Elementary School Journal, 90*, 99–110.

*Teacher Expectations and Student Achievement (TESA) coordinator manual.* (1993). Downey, CA: Los Angeles County Office of Education.

Thomas, N. I. (1928). *The child in America.* New York: Knopf.

Thorndike, R. L. (1968). Review of Pygmalion in the classroom. *American Educational Research Journal, 5*, 708–711.

Thornton, C. L. (1984). *The effects of family and home environment on teachers' expectations for Head Start children's success in school classrooms* [CD-ROM]. Abstract from: ProQuest File: Dissertation Abstracts Item: 8807956

Tompkins, G. E., and McGee, L. (1983). Launching nonstandard speakers into standard English. *Language Arts, 60*, 463–469.

Tucker, L. A. (1984). Physical attractiveness, somatotype, and the male personality: A dynamic interactional perspective. *Journal of Clinical Psychology, 40* (5), 1226–1234.

Vasquez, J. A. (1990). Teaching to the distinctive traits of minority students. *Clearing*

*House, 63* (7), 299–303.

Vaughan, G. M. (Ed.). (1972). *Racial issues in New Zealand.* Auckland, New Zealand: Akarana Press.

Wagar, W. W. (1963). *The city of man, prophecies of a modern civilization in twentieth-century thought.* Boston: Houghton Mifflin.

Walker, R. N. (1962). Body build and behavior in young children: I. Body build and nursery school teachers' ratings. *Monograph of the Society for Research in Child Development, 27* (3, Serial No. 84).

Walker, R. N. (1963). Body build and behavior in young children: II. Body build and parents' ratings. *Child Development, 34,* 1–23.

Warren, S. T. (1989). *An investigation of self-esteem, self-concept, and scholastic achievement of at-risk ninth-graders involved in the Teacher Expectations and Student Achievement (TESA) program classroom* [CD-ROM]. Abstract from: ProQuest File: Dissertation Abstracts Item: 8920981

Weber, B. J., and Omotani, L. M. (1994). The power of believing. *Executive Educator, 16* (9), 35–38.

Weeks, R. C. (1986). *The effects of modifying teacher interaction skills on student behaviour in different ability class* [CD-ROM]. Abstract from: ProQuest File: Dissertation Abstracts Item: No number available

Weinstein, R. S. (1984). *Final report: Ecology of student's achievement expectations* (Grant NIE-G-80-0071). Washington, DC: National Institute of Education.

Weinstein, R. S., Marshall, H. H., Sharp, L., and Botkin, M. (1987). Pygmalion and the student: Age and classroom differences in children's awareness of teacher expectations. *Child Development, 58* (4), 1079–1093.

Weinstein, R. S., Soule, C. R., Collins, F., Cone, J., Mehlhorn, M., and Simontacchi, K. (1991). Expectations and high school change: Teacher-researcher collaboration to prevent school failure. *American Journal of Community Psychology, 19* (3), 333–363.

West, C., and Anderson, T. (1976). The question of preponderant causation in teacher expectancy research. *Review of Educational Research, 46,* 185–213.

Wetzler, J. J. (1986). *A follow-up study to determine if teachers trained in "teacher expectations and student achievement" interact with students more than teachers not trained* [CD-ROM]. Abstract from: ProQuest File: Dissertation Abstracts Item: 8627531

White-Hood, M. (1994). Pride, heritage, and self-worth. *Schools in the Middle, 3* (4), 29–30.

Williams, F., Hopper, R., and Natalicio, D. D. (1977). *The sounds of children.* Englewood Cliffs, NJ: Prentice-Hall.

Willis, S. (1991). The complex art of motivating students. *ASCD Update, 33* (6), 1, 4–5.

Wilson, G., and Nias, D. (1976). Beauty can't be beat. *Psychology Today, 10* (4), 96–98, 103.

Wineburg, S. S. (1987a). Does research count in the lives of behavioral scientists? *Educational Researcher, 16* (9), 42–44.

Wineburg, S. S. (1987b). The self-fulfillment of the self-fulfilling prophecy. *Educational Researcher, 16* (9), 28–37.

Woehr, G. H. (1986). *An investigation of the Teacher Expectations and Student Achievement program* [CD-ROM]. Abstract from: ProQuest File: Dissertation Abstracts Item: 8611945

Yamagata-Noji, A. A. (1987). *The educational achievement of Japanese-Americans* [CD-ROM]. Abstract from: ProQuest File: Dissertation Abstracts Item: 8729392

Zanna, M. P., Sheras, P. L., and Cooper, J. (1975). Pygmalion and Galatea: The interactive effect of teacher and student experiences. *Journal of Experimental Social Psychology, 11* (3), 279–287.

Zuckerman, M., Hodgins, H. S., and Miyake, K. (1993). Precursors of interpersonal expectations: The vocal and physical attractiveness stereotypes. In P. D. Blanck (Ed.), Interpersonal expectations: Theory, research, and applications (pp. 194–217). Cambridge, England: Cambridge University Press.

# INDEX

DR. ROBERT T. TAUBER, Professor of Education at The Behrend College of The Pennsylvania State University, is certified as a physics teacher, guidance counselor, principal, and superintendent. His more than thirty years' teaching experience includes teaching at an inner-city junior high, counseling at a vocational-technical high school, and teaching courses in educational psychology, foundations of education, human development and family studies, and psychology at the university level. Dr. Tauber has supervised student teachers at both the elementary and secondary levels, and for more than twenty years has set up, supervised, and evaluated off-campus field experiences for his educational psychology students.

He has authored five books, including a highly rated classroom management book, and published more than fifty articles in national and international journals. Most recently, he served a six-month sabbatical at the University of Melbourne studying classroom management practices in Australia. Prior to that, he served a year-long sabbatical at Durham University investigating how British educators wield power and influence in the classroom. Dr. Tauber has delivered many scholarly presentations at regional, national, and international conferences, and also regularly presents workshops and seminars to school teachers and administrators.

ISBN 0-275-95502-8

90000>

EAN

9 780275 955021

HARDCOVER BAR CODE